MARIA PASQUA

A Greek Captive by Henriette Browne

MARIA PASQUA

BY MAGDALEN GOFFIN

Oxford London New York

OXFORD UNIVERSITY PRESS

1979

Oxford University Press, Walton Street, Oxford OX2 6DP

OXFORD LONDON GLASGOW
NEW YORK TORONTO MELBOURNE WELLINGTON
KUALA LUMPUR SINGAPORE JAKARTA HONG KONG TOKYO
DELHI BOMBAY CALCUTTA MADRAS KARACHI
IBADAN NAIROBI DAR ES SALAAM CAPE TOWN

© Magdalen Goffin, 1979

British Library Cataloguing in Publication Data
Goffin, Magdalen
Maria Pasqua.
1. Pasqua, Maria
942.081'092'4   CT788.P/   78-40786
ISBN 0-19-211754-8

Set, printed and bound in Great Britain by Cox & Wyman Ltd.,
London, Fakenham and Reading

*This is my mother's book
and is dedicated to her memory with
the love of all her children*

CONTENTS

LIST OF PLATES	ix	TEN	78
FOREWORD	xi	ELEVEN	85
PROLOGUE	1	TWELVE	93
ONE	6	THIRTEEN	99
TWO	16	FOURTEEN	106
THREE	28	FIFTEEN	115
FOUR	35	SIXTEEN	122
FIVE	41	SEVENTEEN	128
SIX	51	EIGHTEEN	137
SEVEN	57	NINETEEN	149
EIGHT	62	TWENTY	154
NINE	71	EPILOGUE	164

LIST OF PLATES

A Greek Captive by Henriette Browne, 1863
(reproduced by courtesy of the Tate Gallery)　　　　*Frontispiece*

Maria Pasqua by Hébert　　　　　　　　　　　*Facing page* 18

Madame de Noailles as a young woman　　　　　　　　19

Maria Pasqua at the time of her marriage　　　　　　　50

Maria Pasqua in 1879, aged twenty-three　　　　　　　51

Philip Shepheard in 1883　　　　　　　　　　　　　51

Abbots Hall　　　　　　　　　　　　　　　　　114

Erpingham Church　　　　　　　　　　　　　　114

Helena Shepheard, aged seven　　　　　　　　　　115

Phil Shepheard, aged twelve　　　　　　　　　　　115

Samuel Shepheard, aged eight　　　　　　　　　　115

Martin Shepheard, aged five　　　　　　　　　　　115

Helena in 1912　　　　　　　　　　　　　　　　142

Edward Watkin at about the time he met and married Helena　142

Phil in 1914　　　　　　　　　　　　　　　　　142

Samuel in 1916 or 1917　　　　　　　　　　　　　142

Samuel in old age, in the grounds of Abbots Hall　　　　143

FOREWORD

My mother Helena Watkin died on Christmas Eve, 1972, aged ninety. She left me all her personal papers, which included various articles on her childhood together with a manuscript life of her mother, Maria Pasqua. She had written this life in 1952 and sent it to Evelyn Waugh. He was haunted by what he considered to be a unique and poignant story. The suggestions that he made for its improvement and presentation were detailed and proved invaluable when I took up the task after my mother's death. She herself had not felt free to enlarge her book while her brother Samuel Shepheard was alive and still at Abbots Hall, nor indeed, since so much material remained in his possession, would she have found it easy to have done so. But her narrative, augmented by information gathered from many conversations on the subject, has remained the core of the present book.

Samuel Shepheard died in January 1974, leaving the bulk of his estate to charity. His executors, however, kindly allowed my sisters and me to remove those papers which could be of value only to the family. These consisted of letters, diaries, albums, prayer books, bills, school reports, catalogues, photographs, wills and account books, some of which reached back to the eighteenth century. Our time was short, it was the depth of winter, we were working under blackened rafters in an unheated house crammed with objects, some of which had not been moved for almost ninety years while others were scattered over the floor in unbelievable confusion. Many papers which

related to Philip Shepheard's first wife were found in the hay-
loft.

We could do no more than unlock the door of each room and
thrust material haphazardly into large plastic bags just as we
came across it. These bags were taken to my home and placed
in the dining-room. It took over a year to sort out the papers
and to classify them; very much longer to assimilate their
contents, integrate the fresh information with my mother's
manuscript and weave them both into this book.

The story, then, is a true one, based on solid documentary
evidence. Factual and unilluminating as they are, Philip
Candler Shepheard left over fifty volumes of diaries, his son
Samuel fifty-seven, Madame de Noailles two hundred and
forty-eight letters. That is not to speak of the rest of the
material found at Abbots Hall and its outhouses. In a book of
this kind footnotes with source references would have been
plainly inappropriate. On the rare occasions when two versions
of the same story have survived, I have chosen the most prob-
able alternative. Unsupported detail has been confined as far as
possible to background description.

Some problems, however, have been difficult to resolve.
Samuel Shepheard said that he intended to burn his mother's
wedding dress together with the letters which passed between
his parents during their courtship and engagement. At his
death neither dress nor letters were found. It must be assumed
that he carried out his intention, and as a result Maria Pasqua's
true feelings towards her future husband cannot be known for
certain. In this part of the book I have had to depend mainly
upon Philip Shepheard's diaries and what Maria Pasqua told
her children. But what she told her children was by then
coloured by disappointment in her marriage and had to be
balanced, here as elsewhere, by reasonable conjecture based on
knowledge of the people concerned.

Documentary evidence, either personal or obtained from

books I have consulted, has been supplemented by verbal testimony. I have drawn heavily upon the memories, including my own, of those who actually knew Philip Shepheard, Maria Pasqua, their children and household.

It would not be possible individually to name all those people who have so kindly put their particular knowledge at my disposal. I must, however, thank my husband Richard for his help not only in correcting the manuscript but for his expert bibliographical advice. My daughter Richenda copied out and translated the references to her great-grandmother written by Théophile Gautier in *Le Moniteur Universel*, 1863–4, for which I am grateful. I must also thank members of the Mack family, especially Christopher Lake for his genealogical assistance and my cousin Marjorie Dixon who was born at Paston Hall and to whom I owe so much. For the amusing story of 'Madame Etiquette' I am indebted to John Hearsey's life of Marie Antoinette. I should like to acknowledge help given by the public libraries of Bournemouth, Norwich and Tonbridge.

I particularly wish to thank my brother Christopher, the Rt. Rev. Dom Aelred Watkin, Abbot of Glastonbury, who not only put his correspondence with Evelyn Waugh and John Hayward at my disposal but gave me unstinting help, both factual and literary. I am equally grateful to my sisters, Perpetua Ingram, Teresa Chapman and Catherine Davenport for the information they have provided and for their companionship during the two extraordinary days we spent together in that icy, desolate, mice-infested house collecting the family papers before the estate passed into strangers' hands for ever.

Some of the buildings described here no longer exist. Holywell Lodge has been demolished; the Catholic church at Tunbridge Wells where Maria Pasqua's bright face was seen on her honeymoon has been pulled down to make way for a supermarket. Other places still stand but have been altered beyond the immediate recognition of those who once lived in them. The grounds of Bridge House have been sold for the building of bungalows, Abbots Hall separated from its land, its medieval farmhouse and thatched barn, the outhouses demolished, the attics given modern windows, the drive flanked by brick pillars, the gardens rendered neat and tidy. Madame de Noailles's villa in the South of France is, I believe, an hotel. No ghosts linger, no voices speak, all the major characters in this story are dead and beyond harm.

This has not absolved me from my obligation to truth and to justice. The act of selection in itself implies judgement, but I have tried very hard to be fair. If the book is a chronicle of selfishness it is also a tribute to love. Philip Shepheard was not given to expressing his feelings. Once, however, in late middle age, he wrote in the margin of his diary, 'to know all is to be compelled to excuse much'. The occasion for his remark is unknown and of little importance. Let it serve as an epitaph for everyone who appears in the following pages.

Silcocks, 1978.

PROLOGUE

When they were small the children wondered why their mother always looked so sad. Long ago in Paris the same thought had occurred to a French critic. 'Le pourquoi de sa misère,' he had written after standing for some time before her portrait, 'est le secret de sa destinée.'

The children understood little about Paris or pictures and nothing at all about destiny. But they did know that there was something mysterious about their mother, and that her childhood had been very different from their own.

One evening towards the end of the year 1891 they were in the nursery. Outside it was dark, and across the lane the cattle were in their sheds. The low wind which had blown all day over the water meadows had died down and in the stillness there was a suggestion of frost. Downstairs their father was in the gun-room, his long fingers gently running a piece of greasy tow through a barrel. In the back kitchen Nana removed the iron from the stove, spat on it, watched the frothy pool contract before touching it tentatively with the side of her thumb and then turned to deal with a pile of small woollen vests.

The blinds were drawn in the nursery and the lamps lit. Except for a faint gleam, a hint of varnish when the fire burnt high, the edges of the room were in shadow. Only morning would bring to life the custard-covered plum pudding with its crown of holly, the stage coaches, the red-cheeked boy with a hoop, the girl in a black riding habit who so nonchalantly set

I

her horse at a five-barred gate, the peacock in his glory, and all the other bright and beautiful pictures their mother had cut out of magazines and pasted over the walls. Now the lamp was at her elbow and the light fell on her face as she sat on the rocking chair with the baby on her lap. She was absorbed in thought, staring sightless into the fire, her expression even more sad than usual.

Her daughter Helena looked at her and loved her, and as she looked the reason for her mother's sadness came to her in a flash. She ran over and rested her hands on her lap.

'Have you ever been in prison?' she asked. The rocking chair stopped. Her mother looked surprised and then amused.

'Why should you think I've been in prison, darling?'

'Because you always look so sad. Something terrible must have happened.'

'I've never been in the sort of prison you're thinking of,' her mother answered slowly, 'but I've spent many years in another kind.'

Helena was puzzled. She was no nearer understanding exactly what was so strange about her mother, to grasping the meaning of those events which so intimately connected her mother's childhood with Madame. It was Madame who was Helena's godmother and after whom she had been called. It was Madame who dominated their lives from a distance, who had to be reverenced, respected, loved and, above all, thanked.

For this the three children, Helena, Phil and Samuel, would sit round the large oak table in the dining-room. Their father ruled the paper with double lines, their mother helped them with ideas. There were certain things which had to be said and there were some subjects which they knew it was best to avoid. They could thank Madame for the Downs' mutton which in truth they were heartily tired of eating. They could say how pleased their mother was with the reed fence Madame had sent to protect her from the east winds which blew so relentlessly in the cold Norfolk spring. They did not tell her that it already had jagged holes where Phil and Samuel had plucked the longest and strongest rushes for their bow and arrows. On their mother's behalf they could express gratitude for the *pâté de foie gras*, the oysters, and the barrels of sea water in which she was meant to bath every day.

After that there were long pauses. Sitting at its verge, the children would stare at the brown granular expanse of the table, hear the faint tapping of the brittle clematis which even then darkened the windows, and smell the scent of fruit that was to linger in that room, to haunt the nostrils eighty years later long after they were all dead and Samuel's solicitor stood awkwardly with the will in his hand. It was time now, their mother told them, to say something out of their own heads. One of Helena's brothers had made a drawing of a pet robin standing on one leg and had told Madame that he had known it ever since it had been an egg. She was delighted and sent him a whole sovereign, the joy of which was immediately quenched by his father, who impounded the money for use when he was older.

Writing to Madame was tedious enough, but the arrival of a letter from her was a more serious matter. Their mother dreaded it. She used to say that when she dreamed of walking by the side of the sea and dabbling her fingers in the water, then one would surely come. The sight of the large envelope with the letter 'N' embossed in gold and surmounted by a coronet caused an uneasy undertow to flow beneath the apparently smooth surface of the household. If the careless slanting black ink were addressed to their mother then there was not so much to fear, but if their father's name was on the envelope then they knew that something was wrong, that a difficult if not impossible request was about to be made and the consequences would be endless placatory refusals, tactful evasions and a general air of vexation.

The children would silently watch their parents' faces as they examined the letter and discussed its contents. Bits of it would be read aloud. Would it not be a great help if their mother took in one of Padre Agostino's orphans? She could weed the garden and quickly learn to wait at table. Before her arrival Madame would teach her how to prepare an excellent *graine de lin* cough mixture which she herself depended upon at the outset of winter. Perhaps their father would be so good as to make sure that the sheep he was sending to her Eastbourne house included a ram capable of fighting a fox. Would he tell her precisely what the cattle on his estate were fed upon and how much cake they were given? She had just met an expert on cattle-feeding and she would like their father's farm bullocks to be fed in exactly the same manner as the expert advised. On second thoughts it would be more satisfactory if the expert came to see for himself. They could put him up and had only to tell her about the time of trains by return of post.

Madame's influence, however, did not reach out merely from a distance. At stated intervals the entire family had to go and stay with her. Their father hated leaving home and was sulky and bad-tempered for days beforehand. Their mother seemed both pleased and agitated, as if she welcomed the thread which bound her to Madame yet longed to sever it. She would come into the nursery and select for Helena a white cashmere dress and another of cream silk, both made in the Grecian style approved by Madame. Helena's two brothers were given blue blouses and wide knickerbockers. Their mother packed broad-toed and flat-heeled shoes for herself together with white flowing garments of a classical shape.

Nothing about Madame's actual presence lessened the children's awe of her. They saw her after tea when they were told to enter the drawing-room one by one and silently kiss her hand. She sat dressed in emerald brocade on a high-backed chair by the fireplace and held a fan. The children were presented singly. She smiled regally and gazed searchingly, almost passionately, at their faces. What she was looking for was beauty.

Their mother sat remote and very still in a corner with a white shawl draped over her shoulders and a crimson screen placed as a background. Sometimes she loosed her hair and it fell in soft brown waves over her shoulders.

She was very beautiful; by far the most beautiful person the children had ever seen. They had always taken it for granted. Yet her beauty was as much part of her destiny as her sadness and lay at the heart of her strange history.

ONE

On Easter Monday the 24th of March 1856, a group of people entered the baptistry of the cathedral basilica of San Clemente in an Italian town called Velletri. They were poorly dressed and included a dark curly-haired man, a few women and some children. The parish priest was tired after the Holy Week services, the people concerned were obviously unimportant, so the baptism was assigned to a visiting curate. The baby was barely two days old and held in the arms of her godmother.

In the evening the parish priest entered the details in the register using the standard abbreviated Latin of his profession which years later was to be scrutinized by a rich woman in Paris and finally translated by a retired schoolmaster living in Bournemouth. On that day, the priest wrote, a visiting curate had with his permission baptized a child born from legitimately married persons, namely: Domenico Abruzzesi, son of Alosio, and Carolina Marc Antonia, daughter of Salvator, inhabitants of Velletri. The godmother was Anna Maria Ciamella and the child herself, the Latin text continues, was named Pasqua Maria.

Pasqua Maria, Maria Pasqua. An ambiguity, a note almost of doubtful identity, entered the child's life from the very beginning. Some people were to call her by the one name, some by the other. She herself hesitated, today she would be Maria, tomorrow Pasqua, the week after Pasqua Maria and after that Maria Pasqua, until she was trapped eventually by convention and legal necessity.

6

She was called Pasqua because she was born within a few hours of Easter Day and Maria not solely out of courtesy to her godmother but because the feast of the Annunciation of Our Lady fell three days later. She had no surname in the modern sense. Her father, Domenico, simply called himself from the place he came from. 'Abruzzesi' means 'from the Abruzzi'.

The provinces that make up the Abruzzi form an oblong lying north and east of Rome. One of the long sides is bounded by the Sabine mountains and the Campania, the other by the Adriatic. To the north lie Umbria and the Marches, to the south the Molise and the lands stretching towards Naples. At the time of Maria Pasqua's birth the Abruzzi formed the north-ernmost limit of the Kingdom of the Two Sicilies.

The wildest, most mountainous, and until recently the least explored district of the Abruzzi lies on the Romeward side. Here the sharp backbone of the Apennines rises peak after peak into the far distance, forming almost impenetrable barriers between one valley and the next. Sulmona, Scanno, Aquila, Leonessa, Celano, the Gran Sasso – the very names are a litany of the remote, the harsh and the beautiful.

What happened took place so long ago that it is impossible now to know the occupation of Domenico's parents or to establish with certainty where he came from. In the face of the disquiet or polite scepticism of her English listeners, Maria Pasqua used stoutly to maintain that her father's clan was of Saracen origin.

It may be so. About sixty miles from Rome, not far from the place where Horace had his farm, are the Sabine mountains. H. V. Morton has described the district as a wilder, sadder Tuscany; remote, romantic and withdrawn, a place where winding tracks lead to white towns perched high on mountain tops. Some of these are inhabited by the descendants of Saracen marauders of the ninth century, who, cut off from the main body of their thieving compatriots, found refuge in those rocky heights and eventually formed a settlement. Moreover, in the nineteenth century the good looks and picturesque costume of the people made them much in demand as artists' models, for which purpose many of them migrated to Rome for the winter. This fits in with much of what we know of Maria Pasqua's childhood, but conflicts with Domenico's one confident assertion. He claimed to have come from the Abruzzi, and he took his name from the Abruzzi. But although on its borders, the Sabine mountains are not in the province.

Was Domenico in reality descended from the Albanians who had taken shelter in Southern Italy from the Turks? Did he come from the so-called Greek Colony at Abadessa, where the women still preserved the Turkish costume? Or did he trace his descent from the people of Scanno where, ten years before Maria Pasqua's birth, the young Edward Lear was struck by the beauty of the strange turbaned figures wearing bright crimson aprons who glided about the streets, white handkerchiefs concealing all but the eyes?

We shall never know. Something hybrid, exotic and inexplicable attached to Maria Pasqua to the end of her life. What her father's origins were she could not tell.

Her mother, Carolina, came from a more conventional background and a less savage landscape. Velletri is a town about thirty miles south of Rome, in those days just within the Papal States and a stage on the road between Rome and Naples. It is a beautiful place, still surrounded in part by crumbling medieval walls beyond which the vineyards stretch out to the slopes of the foothills. The women of Velletri were reputed to be very good-looking. It was here that Raphael saw a lovely mother with her child and asked her to pose for him. He had no canvas and could not even find a scrap of paper, so he did a sketch on the top of a barrel and used it afterwards for the *Madonna della Seggiola*.

Carolina had returned to her parents for the birth of her

fourth child and only daughter. She was herself a woman of striking appearance with bronze-coloured hair and deep blue eyes. But while Maria Pasqua always spoke of Domenico with fierce love mingled with reproach, she never once referred to her mother with affection. It seems that Carolina was domineering, and that because her family owned a bit of land she considered herself to be a cut above her nomadic and feckless husband. As her dowry she brought with her a share in a vineyard. Through either laziness or mismanagement Domenico failed to make it pay and it had to be sold. There was no work and no security. Carolina was forced to accept the uncertain life of her husband's people.

What Maria Pasqua remembered of her early childhood she remembered vividly but unconnectedly, like a landscape illuminated by flashes of lightning. She had no recollection whatsoever of Velletri. She knew only that in winter her parents earned their livelihood as artists' models in Rome, and that in the summer she, her three brothers and her mother and father joined the rest of his tribe on the mountain tops and made their home in the ruins of old palaces and castles.

It may be that Domenico was the only human being Maria Pasqua was ever able unreservedly to love. Certain it is that she looked back upon her early childhood in the mountains as the one real experience of her life. It was the yardstick of all pleasure, the sole measurement of joy, a lost paradise to which she must return as surely as a river runs into the sea. She would describe to her children what she had felt and seen with such vivid imagery, immediacy and emotion that they were transported over the flat landscape outside the nursery window, carried far over the Alps to a land of sun and singing, of high peaks and rushing streams. The tale was told over and over again, and still her children longed to hear more.

Domenico's family did not set out for the mountains until the snows melted in the spring. On the lower slopes the white oxen pulled the plough and wild parsley covered the iron crosses in the village churchyards. Maria Pasqua remembered the almond and olive orchards, the taste of goat's milk, the feel of loose stones under her bare feet and the shadows of the clouds over the barren earth. She remembered too the warmth and how, when she was tired, her father or one of her brothers took turns to carry her.

The climb was long, particularly for children, the final part difficult and exhausting. Eventually the track dwindled, spread out and vanished. Before them were the crumbling walls and the empty windows of the ruin they made their home. Maria Pasqua described their refuge as a temple. It was more likely to have been a deserted castle or a great house in an abandoned town.

On one side their home looked down the sheer face of the mountain to the valley below. So high were they that houses, vineyards and people appeared as they might to the eye of the eagles which soared in the blue sky above them. The other side was open. It looked across one mountain range after another to a single inaccessible peak which never lost its mantle of snow and the memory of which, in later years, became for Maria Pasqua the symbol of all she had forfeited and all she most desired.

The women wore their traditional costumes of blue and pink petticoats with a striped border and strings of bright coral round their necks. They carried a stiletto in their hair and were taught very young how to use it. The men had black hats with peacocks' feathers and wore red waistcoats. Few strangers came near as they could be a violent people. Some of them were still brigands, petty peasant raiders or ruffians who hired themselves out in bands to the highest bidder. Geography had made them independent: they had lived over the centuries under many governments, and cared for none.

But above all they were deeply religious, and in a manner

hard to explain to those accustomed to live in a world where the spirit laps only at the edges of human experience. For Domenico's people religion was as much a part of life as breathing. However crudely interpreted, the consciousness of God's presence was everywhere vivid.

One of the great events of the summer was the procession down the mountains to the shrine below. All the different clans met in their various costumes, singing and playing the bagpipes. The priest knew his mountain flock well.

On one such occasion something happened which distressed Maria Pasqua deeply. The procession took place as usual. The priest with his buckled shoes, his crimson cloak trimmed with fur and pale blue embroidered stole carried the monstrance under the golden umbrella. Behind him, standing on a wooden platform and swaying precariously on the shoulders of his bearers, came a life-size statue of the saint. It ended by all kissing a relic.

Domenico knelt with Carolina at his side, followed by his three sons and Maria Pasqua. When his turn to kiss the relic arrived, however, the priest looked at him, paused, and then passed him over. Domenico burst into tears and sobbed all the way home. His little daughter was shocked and indignant. She never knew what he had done to deserve such a public rebuke.

Life was hard: there was little to eat, clothes were scarce, and when the sudden storms of thunder and hail swept over the mountains the children were cold. But the sun soon dried them and they would run and sing and play again. The very first thing Maria Pasqua remembered was the sound of the pipes.

The children ran barefooted up and down the mountainside and along the edges of the precipices. They learnt to be as surefooted as goats. No one bothered them or taught them anything. They were part of the wild life around them and drank in unconsciously the beauty of their surroundings. Maria Pasqua remembered the chestnut groves and delighted to recall the sound of the water falls with the maidenhair fern hanging above them.

Winter set in early. When October came and in the valley below the almonds looked thin and ragged and the leaves of the chestnuts had turned from yellow to red, they prepared to abandon their home to the birds and animals which found shelter there from the bitter weather. Soon the streams would become rushing torrents and an icy wind whistle through the mountain passes. It was time for them to pack up, to pick their path slowly downwards and by stages make their way to Rome.

The peasants from the Abruzzi lived in the slums of the city. Most of them earned their bread naturally and unashamedly as beggars. There was little else for them to do.

Maria Pasqua never described the conditions of her life in Rome nor later in the slums of Paris. It was not that she was ashamed, rather that she was reluctant to destroy something precious. At the time she accepted extreme poverty as natural. She learnt otherwise at the price of captivity and betrayal. She did not explain that her home was little more than a dark cave with an uneven floor oozing with slime, that the walls were green with mould, that the people and the place stank of olive oil and sour bread, that she was cold and hungry and the children slept on the ground. Instead she spoke of the sound of the *pifferari* at Christmas with their flutes and pipes, of sitting outside in the sunshine of early spring, of shouting across the street and running to receive the blessing of Pope Pius IX as he came among the poor of the city.

Her parents were not beggars. They did not have to depend for their bread upon the possession of a withered arm or one leg. They were paid by the session to pose for artists in their studios. Dickens vividly described the employment exchange for models on the Spanish Steps. Here, on the steep flight leading from the Piazza di Spagna to the church of the Trinita del Monte, sitting, sleeping, eating, men and women together, young and old, the models waited to be hired. Their faces, disguised as St. John the Baptist, the Apostles, Ganymede or Orpheus with his lyre, were familiar to frequenters of art galleries the world over.

Domenico and Carolina were in regular employment. Domenico's good looks made him much in demand as a model for Christ, but he did not remain in his profession long enough to become like the character with the white hair and an immense beard who was known as Padre Eterno from his constant posing as God the Father. The future was to render such prolonged exertion unnecessary.

When Maria Pasqua was five-and-a-half years old Carolina returned to her parents' house at Velletri with her three sons, leaving her husband and daughter behind. Why she went or what made her leave the child with her father, we do not know. Perhaps she and Domenico had had a violent quarrel. Perhaps she was tired of posing or disgusted with the conditions in which her husband's people lived. She may have been expecting another baby.

Whatever the reason, Carolina unwittingly laid the first step in the path that was to take Maria Pasqua out of her life altogether. Instead of leaving her at home, Domenico now brought the child with him to the studios. They were inseparable.

While he stood motionless under the cold light of the high north windows, she would sit on the floor well out of the artist's way and with discarded brushes sweep the dust into minute piles or thrust her little fingers into empty paint bladders. Sometimes the door would open and a hand beckon her down to a warm kitchen where she would be fussed over, given macaroons and allowed to play with the cat. The usual session lasted four hours. When it was over they would return home together, stopping at the street corner to buy roast chestnuts from the stall of a pock-marked friend of Domenico's.

Maria Pasqua's features, however, were forming, and she was not likely to escape notice in a world where faces, and expressions on faces, were bought and sold. Some artist asked her father whether he would allow his daughter to sit for him. Domenico was delighted. The suggestion flattered his vanity and might fill his purse.

For Maria Pasqua it was quite different. Something went out of her life never to return. From that moment she lost her freedom, became an instrument for others to use, an object to be manipulated. She had to behave like a grown-up person, to sit still for hours at a stretch, adopt an attitude chosen by another and abandon it should it fail to serve.

She was a gentle child and wanted to please. Her success was great. The large blue eyes set far apart in the little oval face already had a wistful look, and artists clamoured to paint her.

The strain told. Sometimes she would fall asleep while she was being painted and be unable to sustain her pose. Sometimes her arm went numb and she cried. She became pale and listless. Domenico was distressed. Voluble and amusing, possessed of a natural artistic appreciation, he took it for granted that his daughter would enjoy the life as much as he did. Besides, he had other ideas for her.

Sometimes, like many of their compatriots, they posed for French artists, probably at the Académie de France. It may have been there, at the Villa Medici, where the ilexes shade the garden and the view stretches far away from the city to the faint blue of his home in the distant Apennines, that Domenico first heard the suggestion which, when acted upon, was so drastically to alter Maria's life. Why was not the little girl taken to join the Italian colony in Paris? With a face like that she was bound to be a success.

Why not indeed? If the pair of them had done so well in Rome, what might they not achieve in France? There money was plentiful, the country was ruled by an emperor, the streets were broad enough to allow four carriages to ride side by side without touching each other.

Rome was emptying. When Maria Pasqua begged to be allowed to join her brothers in their refuge in the mountains Domenico readily agreed. But it was the last time.

In the late summer of 1862, when she was six years old and before the snows blocked the passes of the Alps, they started out on their long journey together. Maria Pasqua was never to see Italy again.

TWO

Years later Maria considered that the consequences of this journey destroyed her entire life and happiness. But she looked back upon the doing of it, the time she spent on the road with Domenico, the adventure itself, with nothing but pleasure. She trusted her father absolutely, enjoyed his company, was accustomed to physical hardship and had no notion that they were doing anything unusual. She had very little idea where they were going, why they were going, or how long it would take them.

In those days there were no railway links between Italy and France, and the first effective tunnel under the Alps was not to be completed for another ten years. If Domenico had wished to avoid crossing the Alps with so young a child, it would have been possible for him to have gone to Genoa and from there by sea to Marseilles; or he could have taken the coastal road by Nice and reached Paris via Marseilles and Lyons. This would have taken very much longer, and there is no reason to suppose that he did not decide on the straightforward route. It is easy to exaggerate both the time taken to travel in the past and the dislike people had for it. What is unavoidable is accepted.

It is true that bad weather could make the actual passage over the Alps difficult and dangerous, and that it was always tedious. Passengers had sometimes to travel in the dark through narrow cuttings with walls of snow on either side fifteen feet high, and for the descent to transfer in a freezing wind on to horse-drawn sledges. Continental diligences were bigger and heavier than English coaches and, at the places where they could go forward only very slowly, were frequently attacked by brigands. This meant, in the absence of government guards, the added expense of the hire of outriders.

Such an extravagance would never have occurred to the travellers. Domenico was extremely poor. Whatever the takings of his profession, he had not the temperament to save and could not possibly have afforded a diligence. It is plain from Maria's memories that they hitch-hiked from Rome to Paris, most likely taking the common trade route through Mt. Cenis or the Little St. Bernard. When they failed to get a lift, they walked.

Domenico was a plausible beggar and a cunning thief. He would enter a village hand-in-hand with Maria, put down his pack, take out his *piffaro* and with it a small tambourine which he gave to Maria. When he was tired of piping he would sing, and when he was tired of singing he would dance and she would stand there, too shy to do more than fix her eyes upon him and shake her tambourine in time with his movements. Soon a crowd would collect, Domenico's exertions would momentarily increase and then slow down. This was the signal for Maria to go round from group to group and hold out her tambourine.

Italians love children. They gave generously to the grave-faced little girl who was travelling so far to seek her fortune. Often they invited them both into their homes for a meal or the night, with an offer to go the next twenty miles the following day in the company of the cheeses, the vegetables and the casks of oil. If nothing turned up the pair would sleep in the open by the side of the road to be ready to catch the first wagon which passed in the morning.

She must have been cold, Maria Pasqua's children would say, cold and miserably hungry. She was never cold, their mother would tell them, except in Rome in the winter, and as for being hungry, they did not understand that the poor expect to be hungry for most of their lives: it is only tame rabbits whose stomachs are always full.

If Domenico could not beg enough money for food, he would steal it. He was adept at knocking into market stalls and swiftly pocketing one fallen cheese while offering another to the irate shop-keeper with a bland smile. He could pounce on a stray village fowl as quick as lightning, tuck it under his coat and wring its scraggy neck as soon as they were out of sight. Sometimes they would put up at country inns, primitive places with straw on the floor where the price of a bed was almost nothing. Domenico would sit talking and drinking far into the night while Maria would fall asleep under the table in the company of the dogs and wake up next morning surprised to find herself in a bed.

Their progress must have been slow. We do not know where they left Italy, nor how long they took to complete their journey. As yet Domenico spoke only the smattering of French which he had picked up from his employers in Rome. It is a tribute to his abilities that he was able, without mishap, to bring a child of six in the manner he did across such a long stretch of foreign country.

The Paris which they reached at last was the brittle cosmopolitan capital of Napoleon III, with its geometrical circles and boulevards, buildings glittering with gas light, gilded ironwork and sheetglass. For the moment such grandeur was no concern of the travellers. They went straight to rooms among their own people near the rue des Boulangers.

Domenico was delighted and expansive. How cheaply they had come, a mere nothing, people were so kind when one knew how to manage them. Look at Maria, she'd soon pick up. In Rome there had been a stampede to paint her, he might even have to ration her services. Yes, really, one had to be fair and he was the last man in the world to tire a child. There would be

18

Maria Pasqua by Hébert

Madame de Noailles as a young woman

no hanging about the fountain in the Place Pigalle for his little
Maria Pasqua, nor for himself either, if it came to that.

Nor was there. One of the most astonishing aspects of Maria
Pasqua's life was the speed with which she found her brief
fame. No doubt Domenico was an excellent impressario. He
had push, a glib tongue, and great charm. But the truth of the
matter was that he was lucky. He had come to the right place,
at the right time, with the right child.

However frail the foundations of the Empire would prove
to be, on the surface Paris was then far removed from the
broken city of the next decade. The middle classes were
prosperous and able to patronize the arts on a lavish scale.
Discrimination will always be the prerogative of the few, and
mediocrity triumphed. The majority of painters were as ob-
sessed by the suitability of a certain kind of subject matter as
were their clients.

Pure landscape, portraits of unknown people or pictures of
an ordinary domestic kind were not generally regarded as
proper subjects. What was admired were noble themes, histor-
ical pictures in the grand manner and contemporary scenes
which told their own story. There was an insatiable demand for
genre pictures of a romantic and nostalgic type. For this Maria
Pasqua was admirably fitted. The fact that Paris was at this
time the centre of creative experiments which were to revo-
lutionize the world of art was irrelevant. Her success lay in con-
forming to public taste, not violating it.

Domenico was not slow to describe the rigours of their
journey together, their poverty, the utter dependence of the
motherless child upon his efforts, her success in Rome. Within
six months his gamble had succeeded beyond his wildest
dreams. According to the author and critic Théophile Gautier,
when the Salon opened in 1863 Maria was exhibited, under
various guises, seven or eight times. She was sculpted at least
once.

Today people have so much to distract them that it is hard to grasp the enormous entertainment value the Salon possessed for all classes in nineteenth-century Paris. The exhibition had moved from the cramped grandeur of the Louvre to more spacious quarters at the Palais de l'Industrie in 1855. Here, amid the banks of hydrangeas, fuchsias, camellias, plush sofas and the tinkling of artificial waterfalls, the pictures could be seen by as many as fifty thousand people a day.

Large entrance fees were charged for two hours on weekday mornings. This was the leisurely, fashionable time for viewing, an opportunity to show off clothes, to rub shoulders with the rich, to gossip with the critics, the artists and even with the models, some of whom would draw attention to themselves by posturing near their likenesses. The rest of the day was cheaper and on Sunday the entrance was free. Then, Zola remarked contemptuously, a whole army would invade the place, 'the rearguard of the lower classes, ignorantly following their betters and filing wide-eyed through this great picture shop'.

For the artists themselves that was the most important part of the exhibition. The Salon was almost their sole means of approaching the public, of advertising their wares and effecting a sale. That was why even dissident artists like Corot, Courbet and Manet could not afford to ignore it and why, in the very year of Maria Pasqua's success, there was an attempt to escape from the tyranny of the selectors by forming a rival Salon de Refusés.

Paris was full of Italian models. Maria Pasqua's youth, however, the long journey she had undertaken, her enormous vogue, the uncertainty about her later fate, combined with the fact that at least three of the artists who painted her were eminent academicians, made sure that her short-lived triumph did not go unrecorded.

'The Salon of 1863', wrote the biographer of the popular

painter, Jalabert, 'marked another success. A little Italian called Maria Pasqua had come to Paris with her father; very intelligent and interested in everything. She was used as a model by a large number of painters. Later she was adopted by a lady from Montpellier and educated at a convent at Nîmes. After that all trace of her has been lost.'

Jalabert was fascinated by her. Above all he wanted to capture the expression on her face, the look in the eyes described by a contemporary as both thoughtful and proud. He found it elusive. 'Will you thank my father for the understanding and sensitive way he refers to little Maria,' he wrote home despondently. 'Here in Paris spirituality and delicacy of expression and gesture don't count. Colour, form, and technique are everything. Clever talk is understood but the language of the soul falls on deaf ears.'

He painted her twice, not without difficulty. 'Up to the present,' he wrote, 'my little Italian doesn't satisfy me at all, although I'm determined not to give up whatever happens. One seldom has the satisfaction of getting hold of such a model.' For one picture he dressed her as a peasant child standing by a wall and grasping an apple. In another he portrayed her strolling down the street, in the rather sugary words of his biographer, 'holding a piece of bread in little hands whose fingers are entwined with graceful simplicity. Her blue eyes are lost in thought and reverie.'

The artist called this picture *Maria Abruzèze*. He gave it as a present to the son of Achille Fould, the Emperor's Minister of Finance, who was delighted. 'I go and look at her every five minutes. In fact, I've never had anything which has given me so much pleasure. You don't wish me to thank you, so I will not do so. But I am everlastingly grateful to you for the joy which will always be mine when I gaze at the little Italian whose history adds to her charm.'

The biographer of the artist Ernest Hébert got hold of a

garbled version of the tale. 'In 1864', he wrote, 'the curious adventure of Maria Pasqua took place. She was a little girl of six. The Marquise de Noailles, charmed by the picture, came to see the model and adopted her. Later an English doctor came to attend her, fell in love and married her.'

Ernest Hébert was one of the most distinguished and fashionable painters in Paris. His career was one of uninterrupted success from the time he won the Grand Prix de Rome at the age of twenty-two to an old age loaded with honours. One of his best known pictures, *La jeune fille au puits*, exhibited at the same time as his study of Maria Pasqua, was bought by the Empress Eugénie. Hébert had no sympathy at all for the innovators. 'I'm glad to thank you for your article on Courbet. Manet and Monet,' he wrote to his friend Théophile Gautier, 'It's certainly time that a protest appeared against these gods of filth.' Although he is recognized as a painter of considerable talent in the classical tradition, his conservatism detracts from his reputation, as does his obsession for painting sad, not to say sickly, young women, thus justifying his critics' accusation that he cared only for the pretty and the sentimental. He seized upon Maria Pasqua's naturally wistful expression and turned her into a melancholy, almost tragic, little figure.

His picture shows her sitting down, looking dejectedly in front of her and idly playing with a piece of red wool. The eyes, although beautifully shaped, are far too large for the tiny face; the mouth droops. The expression has none of the vitality and hint of defiance which Jalabert perceived and reproduced in his child holding an apple. Gautier admired it tremendously. 'Monsieur Hébert', he wrote in his newspaper column, 'has conveyed with delicious poetry this wild, childish individual of such primitive grace . . . The eyes have the intense southern gravity which creates such an effective contrast to the young face and the mouth blooms like a large red flower against its smooth whiteness.'

The portrait was extremely popular and crowds jostled to see it at the Salon. It was bought by Baron James de Rothschild for his château at Ferrières, but unfortunately in 1872 a fire destroyed a portion of the picture gallery and the canvas was lost. According to Maria Pasqua herself, however, an engraving had been made of it which was sold under the description 'Mignon regrets her native land'. A few years after painting this picture Hébert took up the position of Director of the Ecole de Rome, working in a studio half hidden by laurel trees in the same gardens of the Villa Medici from whence his little model had ventured out.

Léon Bonnat was a southerner from Bayonne. As a young man he had studied in Madrid and Rome and painted vigorous interpretations of biblical and classical scenes. His 'Christ on the Cross' hung in the Palais de Justice. Later he enjoyed an enormously high reputation as a portrait painter. It was said that a person had not only to be a millionaire but to be recommended by a Minister of State before Bonnat would consent to paint him. When he died in 1922 *The Times* referred to him as a painter of genius, 'bringing a warmth of colouring and an intensity of life which quickly won him recognition . . . His portraits include the delightful *Maria Pasqua*.' This picture was bought by Gautier and is now in the Bonnat museum at Bayonne.

She was painted so often that there must be many unrecorded and unidentified pictures of Maria Pasqua scattered about Europe and America. The most beautiful and perhaps the one most in accord with modern taste was bequeathed to the Tate Gallery in London and used to hang in the French Room there. It was painted by Henriette Brown, Madame Jules de Saux, under the title of 'A Greek Captive'. No one looking at it would imagine that the model was only seven years old. She is wearing a light blue dress with sprigged flowers and a broad red sash. She has a wreath of myrtle in her hair and another on her lap.

Unfortunately Maria Pasqua's actual world was closer to that depicted by Daumier than it was to the romanticism of those who painted her. In a colder climate, she lived in conditions which were little better than those she had left behind her. The gulf between the rich and the poor was then so great that each might have inhabited different planets. When circumstances radically changed Maria's life, what struck her was not the comfort of other people's existence but its strangeness.

In Paris she slept on a mattress on the floor sharing a room with many others. She ate Italian food brought from the market by her landlady, and if she and her father were out of work they went to bed hungry. She expected nothing else, she knew nothing else. According to the weather and the distance they had to go, she and Domenico would either walk or, for a few centimes, travel together on the outside of a horse-drawn omnibus.

At the studios no one was ever unkind to her. Sometimes she was petted as she had been in Rome, given hot chocolate or Savarin cake. Once a model dressed as Persephone produced some sticks of angelica folded in oiled paper. But her presence was a business arrangement. She was there for one purpose only, to be painted. She was hired to be stared at, manipulated, dressed up and expected to remain absolutely still for long stretches at a time. The more she was looked at, the less she existed in her own right. For de Curzon she was seated on a stool by a spinning-wheel. For Bonnat she lay on the floor. Sometimes she stood on the platform in a fixed pose, holding one of the ropes that dangled from the ceiling.

The world of a busy artist in no way struck her as odd. She was used to lofty rectangular rooms, to skylights and palette scrapings, to the iron stove with its ugly pipe, stacks of canvasses marked with chalk, the smell of paraffin, soft soap and tobacco, suits of armour, military uniforms, swords, togas, mangers and shepherds' crooks. For her the trappings of make-believe meant a plate of spaghetti.

Some fashionable painters considered untidyness to be the mark of failure. They worked in a studio, often a room in their home, which they attempted to make as elegant as possible with well-upholstered chairs, pot plants and other people's masterpieces on the walls.

Such places paid better but did not suit Domenico. The silent artist, the ordered establishment, cramped his spirit. Dressed now in a respectable dark suit with a necktie, he liked nothing more than to sit on a packing case with a glass of wine, watch Maria as she sat quietly with her face turned away, get up to advise on the light or the exact positioning of the ribbon in her hair, gossip with students, flirt with a young model just up from Nemours, or slip out to enjoy a quick vermouth at Dinochau's on the corner of the rue Bréda.

If Maria Pasqua was older than she had been in Rome, more was expected of her. It was all very well for Gautier to refer so airily to the delightful, charming little model who sat for her portrait over and over again without complaining. The stress began to tell, and now there were no mountains to go to, no escape with her brothers to the high eyrie in the hills. At some time during the winter of 1863–4 when she was walking in the street with Domenico she stumbled and fell. Frightened, he half pushed her, half carried her to the side. Propped up against the railing, her head lolled forward like an empty puppet. A small crowd gathered. She was dying of cold. She must be starving. She had a fever. Perhaps it was typhoid. Where was her mother? She must be taken to hospital. She had no home, Domenico said, nor a mother. He would look after her, he always had, he could manage, provided of course, he had a little help. He took her in his arms and enquired the way to the house of the Sisters of Charity.

Maria Pasqua must have been very ill, for she stayed at the

Convent for some months. The nuns were extremely good to her and she never forgot them. For the first time in her life she was living in an ordinary house. For her, the plain rooms and the iron bedsteads spelt luxury. She was clean, warm, secure, given regular meals and, above all, no demands were made upon her. She looked back upon those months as the happiest time she spent in Paris. She had never played like other children, and the nuns had to show her what to do with toys. They taught her to knit, to use scissors and to work with Berlin wool. She ran about the garden and played ball with the other children. She was safe, Domenico was in Paris, he would come in his own time.

Come he did. One day she heard, from the street outside, a melody she at once recognized; repetitive, simple, and haunting. She rushed to the window and there on the pavement she saw her father playing gaily on his *piffero*. She knocked wildly on the glass but he did not hear; he was absorbed in his music, his head tilted on one side as if, in brown blanket coat and pointed hat, he was playing at some mountain shrine.

The nuns were reluctant to let her go. They did not approve of her way of life and feared for her future. They tried to persuade Domenico either to take her back to Italy or to allow her to be trained for respectable work. They had a host of connections, many ladies visited them who would be only too glad to find her a suitable place in their own homes. Domenico laughed. He couldn't part from Maria. She wasn't going to be a servant. She was coming with him. She was one of the cleverest and loveliest little creatures in Paris and who knew where she might end up?

The answer to his question was even then being decided. In the May of 1863 a woman had returned repeatedly to the Salon. She stood in the Rotunda staring at Hébert's picture of the child with the great eyes. A scheme for the benefit of a number of people glittered like a spinner on the surface of her mind.

Impulsive in thought, cautious in action, she did not bite immediately. When she did the ripples were to extend in ever widening circles, down the Seine, across the Channel and to the edges of the North Sea.

THREE

Helena, Comtesse de Noailles, was an Englishwoman. She was the daughter of William Gordon Cosvelt and Anna Maria Baring, the half-sister of the first Lord Cromer and the first Lord Revelstoke. In 1849, when Helena was twenty-five, she married Antonin, the second son of Juste de Noailles, Prince-Duc de Poix. The marriage was not happy. Their only child was stillborn and they separated after three years. The Comte died young leaving all his money to a natural son but, as a Baring, Madame de Noailles was very rich in her own right.

She had a house in Paris, another in Montpellier, and spent the spring restlessly wandering from hotel to hotel in the South of France. She was a keen patron of the arts, especially of painting. Exceptionally cultivated, she knew Latin and Greek and was very well read in history and literature. She interested herself in all sorts of schemes for social reform, some absolutely impossible, others, like her campaign against the adulteration of food, now almost universally accepted. A sincere philanthropist, she gave away a great deal of money to carefully selected causes and crusades.

Fundamentally she was a good woman, but she was spoilt, autocratic, and self-indulgent in the manner of her class. Her wealth enabled her to give way to her violent temper, to be capricious, exacting, exceedingly eccentric and to gratify any whim she chose.

She had come up from the South of France to attend the

Salon of 1863, and was immediately attracted by the pictures of Maria Pasqua. She studied the catalogue, read Gautier's articles in *Le Moniteur Universel* and heard the stories circulating about the little Italian who had accompanied her father all the way from Rome. She had met Ernest Hébert, and his new picture both delighted and moved her. She thought that the child's magnificent eyes reflected the wisdom of ages, the conscious, uncomplaining acceptance of life upon the terms on which it is offered. She wanted to have the likeness by her always. When she inquired the price she was told that it had been bought already by the Baron de Rothschild.

Returning home she pondered over the final words of Gautier's piece in that day's paper. In Hébert's obstinate attraction for painting Italian subjects, she read, there existed a certain foreboding. 'It seems that the artist, treasuring the old picturesque Italy, wants to preserve the image before it is destroyed by invading civilization. Soon these beautiful girls from such a pure race and with such unblemished character will wear crinolines and hats after the fashion of Paris. Today's ugliness will overcome them and they will exist only in the pictures of M. Hébert.'

Next day Madame de Noailles went back to the Salon again and as she looked at the small hands lying vulnerable, soft, and half-opened on the bright childish apron, she was overwhelmed by the desire to protect, to guide, and above all, to possess. The child would not be overcome by ugliness, she would not exist only in Hébert's picture. M. de Rothschild could keep it. She would have the original.

Lonely, unfulfilled, genuinely loving beauty and wishing to do good, Madame de Noailles returned once more to her house near the Champs Elysées and thought the matter over. The child would, of course, have to be unravelled like a piece of knitting. She must be properly educated, taught manners, schooled to be a fit companion for herself – but all these things could be achieved only by building on a foundation of natural virtue.

The father was poor, he would be willing enough to sell. But she must find out if Maria Pasqua really was his daughter and, if so, whether she was legitimate. She must know who the mother was. She must see the child herself first to make certain that she had not been idealized in order to catch the market at the Salon. She would get in touch with Monsieur Hébert and possibly with her solicitor, who would have to arrange the Italian side of the affair.

The matter proved more complicated and the negotiations more prolonged than Madame had first imagined. Her legal advisors were against the scheme; Hébert furthered it. Maria Pasqua was no longer sitting for him, but he knew the address of Domenico's lodgings. Madame wanted to see the child for herself before she got in touch with the father. Where and how she did so is not known, but she was satisfied. Not until then was Domenico approached, at first indirectly. The proposition was put, but since Madame expected to haggle over the price she thought it wiser for the time being to remain anonymous.

Domenico was surprised and indignant. To adopt Maria? To buy his daughter? Never. She was his little companion, together they had travelled over the Alps, sought refuge in Paris, worked in the studios, and found fame at the Salon. The good Sisters of Charity had offered to find a home for her but he wouldn't hear of it. An Englishwoman? She would be rich then. What did she want of Maria?

Gradually, over many months, while Maria Pasqua was still working at the studios, the truth came out. So it was Madame la Comtesse de Noailles. She would pay a good price.

As Madame had foreseen, Domenico drove a hard bargain. He longed to return to Carolina as a man of substance. He wanted enough money to buy back not merely a share in the vineyard but to become an independent proprietor. Nor would he allow Maria to be taken by Madame in any other capacity than that of adopted daughter. She must be brought up not as a servant, companion, or governess, but as an equal. To this Madame agreed.

Still Domenico hesitated. He could not bring himself to act. He had looked after the child almost exclusively since she was five. They had suffered, endured, been happy together. She was devoted to him, relied upon him, trusted him absolutely. But now the good fortune he had always boasted about had come. Could such an opportunity ever occur again? Maria would be a lady. She would be rich. She was his little Cinderella. She would no doubt marry a nobleman. Left in his care things might get difficult for them. The life of a child model was short. She might not grow up to match the promise of her beauty, and even if she did, to what temptations would she not be exposed? And then he would be the owner of a vineyard. The prospect made him swagger just a little. Carolina's mother would be confounded. It was only right to think of his three sons, too: they would all share in his prosperity. It would be unfair to the whole family to refuse. Yet he could not bring himself to accept, to face the fact of parting.

When he did, Madame was in Cannes. She sent word for her town house to be opened and, accompanied by a maid called Médicis who had been specially employed to look after Maria as she spoke both French and Italian, travelled at once to Paris. There, late on a spring evening in 1865, she sat in her drawing-room and waited.

The importance of the step she was about to take sharpened Madame's perception. Years later, when she was an old lady, she described what happened in detail to Maria Pasqua's daughter, her namesake, Helena.

Madame had left her two black labradors at Cannes, as she thought they might frighten the child. She sat alone in her room on a high backed chair as was her custom. She had told the servant to let Domenico and his daughter straight in without announcing them. The appointed hour came and went. She grew anxious.

Suppose Domenico had changed his mind? At that very moment they might be trudging together across Paris to the Gare de Lyons *en route* for Marseilles and a boat for Genoa. Or, should they come, what if the child proved to be not merely less lovely than her portraits but to have lost that otherworldly expression which Hébert had captured and she had seen herself? She rang the bell for the great gas chandelier in the centre of the room to be lit. Then she ordered the thick velvet curtains to be drawn, shutting out the garden, the scolding of the blackbirds in the shrubbery, and the shadow of the acacia reflected on the green and gold of her walls. She was not an imaginative woman, nor given to doubting her own judgement. She had everything to offer. She feared only that they would not come.

When the double doors opened she was surprised by Domenico's respectable appearance and struck by his good looks. He led Maria Pasqua by the hand and bowed very low. He was wearing a dark suit with a wide necktie secured by a gilt pin. She signalled for them both to sit on the sofa, and when they did she saw to her relief that she had made no mistake about the child. Maria sat very still and stared gravely at Madame. Her father had bought her a new pair of boots, a print bonnet and a blue cloak. All these, together with her underclothes, Madame later ordered to be burnt for fear of infection.

Domenico spoke fluent but not always accurate French with a strong Neapolitan accent. He was very much at his ease and extremely lively, and Madame was quite captivated by his charm. He inquired about her health, complimented her upon her wisdom in having a fire lit on such a chilly evening, asked how the acidity of the Parisian air affected the plants in her garden, and told her that it was well known that the Empress preferred the white wine made from the grapes grown on the slopes near Montpellier to the finest champagne.

So was Madame gently reminded of the business side of their transaction. Domenico had asked for the money to be paid in gold. By Madame's standards it was not much; by his a fortune. She went over to a bureau and took out two washleather bags. As she carried them over, suddenly Maria's loss became more real to Domenico than his vineyard.

His face, with its straight nose and strong teeth, grew tighter and older. Madame must wait, he said. There were two further conditions he must insist upon if he were to entrust his daughter to her care. Madame was, of course, a Protestant, but she must promise to bring up the child in the Catholic faith and give her opportunities to practise her religion. Secondly, she must never allow her to be painted again.

Maria Pasqua understood very little French and could not follow the conversation. She knew they were talking about her, but thought that her father was making arrangements for Madame de Noailles to use her as a model. She had no idea that private houses on such a scale and of such grandeur existed. She thought at first they might be in an hotel, then, when she saw the money bags, wondered if perhaps they were in a bank. She was fascinated by the sparkling, dancing crystals of the chandelier. She looked at it, screwed up her eyes, and then turned back to stare at the tall woman with the high nose who was speaking so earnestly with her father. Yes, Madame had just said: he could depend upon it that she would fulfil his two conditions since they had been her intention in the first place. It was her duty to bring up Maria in the religion of her baptism, and now they were to spend their lives together there was no point in having her painted.

Domenico put one bag in each pocket. Very well, he said, very well. But he must warn her of one thing. The Abruzzesi were never tricked. There were many of his fellow countrymen in Paris and on the Riviera. They would watch and see. If a single one of his conditions were not observed he would return and, if need be, take away the child by force.

He got up and so did Maria Pasqua, as she did so putting her hand in his. At this he burst into a torrent of tears. Madame rang the bell and told Médicis to take the little girl to her room.

FOUR

At first Maria Pasqua did not realize that she would never see her father again. No one wished to tell her or was prepared to overcome the difficulty of doing so since she knew no English whatsoever, very little French, and it turned out that Médicis's Italian was not hers. The child spoke only the local patois of her own people; in the beginning Médicis could hardly make herself understood, Madame not at all. She was as bewildered and as totally disorientated as a captured bird that has been put into a box and released in another place. Gentle and shy by temperament, she was thrust into a world she had no idea existed, and the initial shock was so great that in after years she found it difficult to speak about it.

Maria was nine years old, but up to then her experience had been confined to the lodgings of her family, the studios, and a brief sample of a more regulated life with the Sisters of Charity. She was not used to wearing shoes indoors or to washing daily. For her, changing clothes and brushing hair were not related to cleanliness but to work she was paid for. She had never been accustomed to a bath or a fire in the bedroom, and was used to sleeping in her underclothes. She had never walked up a grand staircase, trodden everywhere on carpets, seen silver, glass, or a table laid for dinner. She had never been waited on by a servant, she did not understand why there were so many people in the house and, above all, she did not know what she herself was doing there.

Sometime after Maria Pasqua had grown up, Madame met

Frances Hodgson Burnett in the South of France. Mrs. Burnett was the enormously successful author of *Little Lord Fauntleroy* and *The Secret Garden*. She shared with Madame a loathing of vivisection, an acquaintance was formed, and Mrs. Burnett was told the tale of Madame's adopted daughter. This she made use of in a story called 'Piccino'.

Maria Pasqua is turned into a little boy as dirty as a pig and as beautiful as an angel, with curls like the Sistine Madonna and eyelashes as thick as rushes. Madame de Noailles is called Lady Aileen and the scene is set in San Remo. Piccino is purchased for the price of the family donkey and taken back to Lady Aileen's villa, where the utterly disgusted servants are instructed to remove and burn his filthy clothes and give him a bath. His reactions are violent. He screams and kicks, refuses to wash, to eat English food, to be dressed up in the clothes provided and to be treated generally as a pretty doll. He insists on sleeping with the dog in his bed and after two days, much to the relief of Lady Aileen, runs off to find his way home.

Since Maria Pasqua was so reticent about certain aspects of her adoption, it is impossible to say how much Mrs. Burnett's description of the child's reaction was imagined and how much was based upon what Madame actually told her. She may have cried. It is doubtful if she attempted to escape. One of Maria Pasqua's most persistent characteristics was an outward submission, a docility, an acceptance, however grudging, of things as they were. The child who had stood for Jalabert hour after hour patiently caressing an apple might resent her pose. She would never abandon it.

Nor was Madame a Lady Aileen. A more unsuitable person to be in sole charge of an intelligent and sensitive child can hardly be imagined, but whatever else might be said about the adoption of Maria it was not merely a capricious and irresponsible use of wealth. Madame's motives, however selfish and peculiar, were rooted in a genuine love of beauty. She bought the child because she was convinced that contemplation of excellence elevated the human spirit. She imagined that when Maria was tamed and taught, cut to shape as surely as a tailor guides his scissors through the cloth, then they would be fit companions for each other. She herself would provide the home, the education, the riches: the child would be devoted, grateful and a constant source of spiritual and aesthetic pleasure.

In fact, Madame grew to love Maria as deeply as she was capable of loving anyone. The child was never able to respond. To the end she remained frightened of her, and in these early years she was absolutely terrified.

Madame was forty: she was set in her ways and did not expect to have her routine disturbed. During the early months Maria was looked after almost entirely by Médicis. It was decided not to speak Italian at all but to concentrate on French. Later, she would be taught English. Maria completely forgot her Italian. She never spoke it again except, as her husband would one day tell her, to murmur it constantly in her sleep. However resentful the other servants may have been at having to wait upon someone whom they regarded as inferior, Médicis was very kind. Maria was given dolls with pale pink dresses, china faces and blue eyes. She loved colour and brightness and would beg Médicis to show her how to make her dolls little aprons with scarlet and green stripes like the ones she had worn for Hébert. Médicis took her to church, taught her to sew, how to use a goffering iron and to make coffee cream fondants.

Madame was accustomed to fall into ungovernable rages when she would shout, scream, and throw things at the servants. Although, to do her justice, she never lost her temper with Maria, she saw no reason to control herself merely because there was a child in the house. Once Madame yelled so loudly that Maria ran wildly from the room, up the stairs to the attics, and hid herself under a bed. She lay there terrified, wedged in

37

a corner in the dust against the wall, hoping she would not be discovered. Madame sent a servant to look for her; eventually she was found and urged to come out. She did not move. Médicis was summoned. Maria still would not come. In the end Madame herself climbed to the top of the house in floods of tears and implored her to emerge. When at last she crawled out from under the bed she was kissed and hugged and her forgiveness asked. This she disliked as much as the screaming.

When they were in Paris Maria longed to have a plant of her own, to water it and watch it grow. At first Madame refused, saying there were plenty of flowers in the garden. In the end Médicis got permission and they bought a little flower in a pot. Maria looked after it with great care and kept it on the window ledge of her room. One day it fell off the ledge and into the street, in its fall slightly injuring a passer-by. Madame scolded Maria and she was forbidden ever to have a plant again. In future years she was to make up for this.

Madame's bedroom had a particular fascination for her. She had never seen such a high and grand bed, nor a looking glass which hinged back and forth so that she was able to catch the reflection of her whole body. What attracted her above all, however, was Madame's dressing-table. It was very tall and on it were various pots of face cream. Maria had been told what they were for and allowed to smell them but warned that on no account must she touch them herself.

One day, when she knew Madame was out, she decided she would go and smell them again. Carefully, she pushed a chair towards the dressing-table, stood on it and reached down. She opened the jars one by one, smelling each and telling herself what was different about them. But the temptation to touch, to dig her little finger in, as long ago in Rome she used to play with the studio paints, was too much for her. She made minute craters and savoured the pleasure of running her nail across an unblemished surface.

That evening Madame de Noailles took note of the damage. She waited until morning and then confronted Maria with her crime. The child was terrified. She thought Madame might start to scream at any moment and denied having been near the bedroom, let alone touching the face cream.

Madame pointed out the wickedness of her lie. Médicis was summoned and told to take Maria to Confession at once. All the way to the church she wondered how she would be able to tell the priest, what he would say to her and if he would be very shocked. When they got there Médicis rang the presbytery bell and they were told to wait in the church. When the priest came he turned out to be a very old man. Choking with tears and trembling with fear, Maria told him of her sin. To her joy, he told her not to worry about Madame in the least and to forget the whole matter. To dry her tears he took her into the garden and allowed her to pick a ripe peach from the orchard wall.

By marriage Madame was allied to one of the noblest families in France. It was not so very long since a former Comtesse de Noailles had accompanied Marie Antoinette to Versailles as a bride and become the nagging 'Madame Etiquette' of the Dauphine's household. Dismissed by Marie Antoinette when she became Queen, poor Madame de Noailles developed a religious mania and imagined she was in direct correspondence with the Blessed Virgin. In this she was encouraged by a sycophantic priest who wrote letters to Madame purporting to come from the heavenly courts. Religious fervour had not, however, diminished Madame Etiquette's knowledge of protocol. In one letter she detected a slip in the form of address which, she explained to her confessor, must only have come about because Our Lady's origins were bourgeois while St. Joseph was descended from the House of David. However, when the hour struck, she followed her former mistress to the scaffold with equal courage and, as she and her daughter passed by on the tumbril, a priest in the crowd risked his life to give them absolution.

Such were some of the French connections of Madame; and Maria Pasqua was expected to conform to a very strict code of manners, as repressive in its way as the discipline of the studios. Nor was another purpose of her adoption forgotten. It is true that Madame kept her word to Domenico. From the age of nine Maria was never painted again. Instead she was treated as a living picture.

The news soon got about that Madame had acquired the little Maria Pasqua. After a certain time had elapsed, invitations to come and look at her were circulated. At a stated hour every week the child was dressed in what Madame considered to be suitable clothes and sent down to the drawing-room. Madame's guests gazed at her from every angle. They took her to the light, pushed back her hair and scrutinized each feature. Since they were very rich, very fashionable, very well bred and not altogether certain of Maria's status, they were also very impertinent.

Madame's sister-in-law, daughter of the old Duc de Noailles, had married into the Standish family. Maria remembered them particularly vividly, not merely because she was then learning English but because they made unusually direct comments on the length of her nose, the breadth of her forehead, and the tilt of her chin as if she were a head of livestock. Madame lapped up their appreciation as they intended she should, but Maria Pasqua began to resent her own beauty. Without it she would never have been bartered for a vineyard, have exchanged the wild waterfalls of the Abruzzi for the tinkling extravagances of the Salon. Once it had seemed natural for her to be looked at. Now she understood what it really meant to be valued not as a person but as an object.

FIVE

Madame de Noailles never stayed long in any one place or country. Together with Maria, Médicis and the others of her suite, she would move restlessly from Paris to Montpellier, Montpellier to Cannes, Cannes to Antibes and back to Paris and across the Channel to Hastings or Bournemouth. In those days the resorts in the South of France were small and frequented by comparatively few. This suited Madame because she disliked casual contact with other people, and in any case was very nervous of infection. For this reason she avoided crowded places and when she travelled took care to do so either by road in her own coach or in a special carriage attached to the train.

Her coach was an extraordinary vehicle which had once belonged to King Louis-Philippe. Drawn by a pair of horses, it was very wide and upholstered in damask. It contained all the luggage and food for the journey, was fitted with a folding bed, a portable lavatory, provision boxes and a sword case. Madame had it taken aboard the Channel steamers and to avoid meeting other passengers, would remain in it herself throughout the crossing.

She had a horror of exposure to the east wind and, however far the preparations were advanced, would postpone a journey should the wind be blowing from that quarter. On one occasion she and her entourage were being seen off by a Miss Ellen Taylor. Miss Taylor was a lady-in-waiting to Queen Victoria's daughter, Princess Alice, Duchess of Hesse Darmstadt. The private coach had been attached to the train, the farewells

made, the guard had blown his whistle, when to Maria's dismay and to the astonished fury of the other passengers,
Madame poked her head out of the window. 'Stop the train!'
she shouted. 'I refuse to go. Take out the luggage.' She had
only just noticed that the wind was in the east. Miss Taylor was
equal to any emergency. She pushed Madame back again into
the carriage and to the relief of everyone made a sign to the
guard to start at once. Madame was furious and said that if she
died of pneumonia and Maria were left motherless again it
would be all Miss Taylor's fault.

She expected the best rooms to be assigned to her at the
hotels she patronized and would not go to sleep until a string
of onions was hung outside her bedroom door. She said that
onions kept away infection. Once she startled the entire hotel
by rushing out of her room in the middle of the night and firing
a pistol. She told the manager that she had seen a burglar.

She was now free to put into practice those educational
theories she had long cherished. She considered that the clothes
worn by most children were exceedingly unhealthy since they
did not allow the air to circulate freely round the body. They
were also ugly, and physical ugliness was a reflection of spiritual
disharmony. Maria was therefore made to wear long tunic-like
garments gathered loosely at the waist by girdles of contrasting
colours. She was allowed to wear nothing but hand-made
sandals, since Madame wished the child's feet to grow as
naturally and as healthily as they would have done had she been
left a peasant in the mountains.

Phrenology was still popular and Madame was a great
believer in the theory that special bumps on the head denoted
certain characteristics. She bought a plaster head with all the
bumps marked on it and was constantly pressing Maria's skull
to see how her lumps corresponded with those on the plaster
cast.

She decided that she did not wish the child to learn Greek and

Latin but to have perfect command of English and French. She was to draw, paint, learn music, history, geography, arithmetic and be thoroughly conversant with the cultural achievements of the civilized nations. Ballroom dancing she thought worldly and shallow but classical dancing encouraged graceful gestures and assisted deportment.

The frequent journeyings of Madame and her entourage from place to place, however, made it very difficult to establish any continuity in Maria's formal education. She was sent to attend lessons at various schools in France but she was always removed before she could settle down.

When Maria was thirteen Madame thought that she would try an English convent. In any case, she wished nuns to prepare Maria for her First Holy Communion. After a great deal of consideration she chose an establishment on the south coast, the Convent of the Holy Child at St. Leonard's.

The experiment was a dismal failure. At first the nuns were pleased to have Madame de Noailles's adopted daughter and went to extraordinary lengths to accommodate themselves to her ideas. Madame insisted that the pond in the school grounds should be drained as she considered stagnant water unhealthy. She arranged for a special cow to be dispatched so that Maria could be absolutely certain of drinking only pure milk. She did not approve of the school uniform and prevailed on the nuns to allow Maria to wear only the Grecian tunics of her design. Nor was she to attend the normal classes which were destructive of individual development and paralysed initiative. She must sit away from the rest of the class and learn grammar and arithmetic according to a system specially devised by herself.

Nothing could have been more conducive to misery. By this time Maria Pasqua had reconciled herself outwardly to her new life. It was no longer incomprehensible. She had made a pattern of it, imposed a kind of order on experience. She realized where Madame de Noailles stood in the scheme of things and where she herself stood in relation to Madame de Noailles. She recognized that she was very fortunate to have been given such opportunities, she was grateful for all she was being taught and told Madame she was happy. But in her heart she longed for Italy and for her freedom. To the end of her life she looked upon Domenico's action as a betrayal and the vineyard as a potter's field. Now, at the Convent, she was once more wrenched out of her environment. Set apart, conspicuous, considered a freak by her companions, she went through torment. Fortunately the end was quick.

Quiet and withdrawn as she appeared in everyday life, Maria was discovered to have a talent for acting. Thinking to please Madame, she was given a large part in the end-of-term play. The child was happy. It was natural for her to dress up in other people's clothes, to assume a different identity, to express emotions which, if she did not feel today, she would tomorrow.

Madame was given a place of honour in the front row with the parish priest on one side of her and a nun on the other. She had a great dislike of the theatre, judging it both frivolous and tending to immorality. She anticipated a pious tale, she found a secular drama with Maria playing the star role. Hissing slightly and tapping with her foot, she contained herself until the interval when she turned on her companion. She was shocked, she said, that the nuns should allow their pupils to make such exhibitions of themselves. Maria's inheritance was uncertain, her early background dubious: suppose her evident success should encourage her to put her beauty at the service of an immoral profession? The play must cease and Maria return home with her at once.

After this there were no more boarding schools. Madame employed outside teachers, a thin French woman called Mademoiselle de Ville, a German girl for music, and Miss Roche for religious instruction.

Miss Roche had long been a most important part of

Madame's household. A poor but well-bred spinster, she was Madame's companion and complete slave. She read to her by the hour, listened to her schemes, and wrote numerous letters at her dictation. She organized her journeys, booked the hotels and tipped the porters. She interviewed servants, bought needlecases at charitable bazaars and poured out the tea. Unfortunately, much to Madame's annoyance, she misunderstood an order and in 1870 missed the last train out of Paris where she had to remain throughout the siege. Madame never failed to reproach her for her folly, she to regale everyone she met with dreadful tales about stewed rats, soup made from leather belts and the great privilege she had had of taking the Blessed Sacrament to those in prison.

On the night of Maria Pasqua's adoption she had been left behind at Cannes to look after the dogs in Madame's hotel. She had not wished the scheme to proceed, thinking the idea foolish in principle and troublesome in execution. Impoverished and utterly dependent herself, when she saw Maria she had pity on her; but the pity was mixed with resentment and a fear that the child would grow up to supplant her in Madame's favour. Yet she was never unkind to her, and as the years passed they faced together the tempests and storms which daily battered the household.

Just before the Franco-Prussian war broke out Madame, who already had two houses in France and several in England, decided to buy another at Meads, near Eastbourne. It was a large rambling house at the foot of the Downs called Holywell Lodge. In those days there were no buildings round it and beyond the garden lay the bare grasslands above Beachy Head. Madame seemed to be happier there than anywhere else; at least she lived there, on and off, for more than twenty years.

Princess Alice, soon to die tragically of diphtheria, used sometimes to take a house at Eastbourne with her young family. One of her daughters, Princess Alix, was to marry the last Czar of Russia, another to be grandmother of the Duke of Edinburgh. They were simply and strictly brought up. Once Maria Pasqua was invited to an afternoon party there. The children were all told not to run about and dirty their dresses until an important visitor who was expected had been properly received. Princess Irene promptly ran out into the garden, rolled over and over on the lawn and got her frock filthy. When her mother saw it she would not allow her to change, telling her that she must accept the consequences of her disobedience and remain in her dirty dress to greet their visitor. The Princess cried bitterly and stationed herself behind Maria, pressing her head against the small of her back in an attempt to hide.

Madame entertained a good deal. She liked to have at her table the type of woman she imagined she herself would have been in different circumstances. There was Barbara Bodichon, the friend of George Eliot, who had laboured so long in the cause of women's education; Miss Blennerhassett who, as Sister Aimée, was later to make a splendid trek through Mashonaland as a medical missionary; Sir Richard Burton's wife, just back from a spell in Trieste; Dr. Elizabeth Blackwell, the first female to show those foolish doctors that a woman could take a medical degree; and Mr. and Mrs. Coventry Patmore.

Madame herself, if not a witty talker, was a forceful and knowledgeable one. Maria learnt as much from the conversation round her as she did from books. Her painful and tedious apprenticeship was over. She had grown up to be small and slight with an oval face, deep blue eyes with dark lashes, and brown hair with red lights. She had a beautiful voice, exceptionally clear, almost bell-like, yet very soft. She spoke English perfectly but with a slight French accent. Her manners were excellent, her deportment graceful, and if she did not wear

Gautier's detested crinoline it was only because it had gone out of fashion. Instead, she stood for hours at Madame's receptions dressed in heavy silk, tight-waisted with a long train carefully arranged behind her.

Madame had kept her word and brought her up as her daughter. But the fact remained that the relationship was one of courtesy and not of blood, of dependence and not of equality. Maria had no money of her own, Madame paid for everything. Her sole possession was her beauty, and that was an ambiguous asset.

Madame was both proud and jealous of her. She was pleased with the girl she had fashioned but fearful lest Maria should attract attention away from herself. If she spoke too much at table she would be snubbed. If any young man showed more than an artistic appreciation of her good looks he was never invited to the house again. Madame was determined not to lose Maria by marriage. If she thought there was the slightest risk of any visitor falling in love with Maria she would be sent to dine alone in her room.

Whether the privations of her early years had weakened her constitution or the strain of living with one who so overshadowed and distorted her personality eventually took its toll, it is hard to say. But when Maria was eighteen she fell seriously ill. Madame was alarmed and sent for her friend Dr. Garth Wilkinson, the Swedenborgian. Dr. Wilkinson summed up the situation. Courageously he told Madame that when Maria recovered it was very important for her to convalesce abroad, in the country of her choice and preferably in the company of someone nearer her own age. Maria asked for her mountains. Madame was convinced that if Maria set foot in Italy again she would be kidnapped by Carolina. Even the South of France was not safe. It was decided that she should go to the Pyrenees. Miss Roche could not be spared. Maria set out for Eaux Bonnes accompanied by a young German woman called Miss

Francken whom Madame employed to play the piano to her. Miss Francken was told to improve Maria's German and to keep men at a distance.

They were gone for two months. Away from Madame, Maria was relaxed and happy. Given the opportunity, she had an enormous capacity for life and experience. She enjoyed the journey; for once there were no tantrums, no fetching and carrying, explanations and raised eyebrows. Madame had chosen well. Maria found herself in a beautiful little town high up in the Pyrenees. The great gorges, the torrential rivers, the magnificent mountain scenery were her birthright. She took the waters, had herself photographed in native costume and laughed again. She was to remember her happiness literally to her dying day.

At first when she got home Maria was well, but next year grew pale and listless once more. Dr. Wilkinson thought she might pick up her strength in Bournemouth could she but find a suitable family to stay with. Madame thought of her dear friend Dr. Compton and his wife: they were elderly, it was true, but they had a large circle of acquaintance.

Although far smaller than it is today, because of its mild climate Bournemouth was a favourite resort for the wealthy and the retired, and a significant number of people wintered there. At that time it harboured a very active Catholic community. This community was rich, aristocratic, cosmopolitan and devout. It was also austere, self-denying and tirelessly devoted to good works.

Among the leaders of this group were the old Baroness von Hügel and her daughter Pauline, the sister of the writer Frederick von Hügel. Pauline was about Maria's age. She was a gifted musician and accomplished linguist, but after her first outwardly brilliant Season in London she decided to abandon society and to dedicate her entire life to God, in the service of others. With this in mind she gave most of her money to the diocese for the building of a new Catholic church and presbytery at Boscombe.

Another prominent member of the group was the well-known novelist and author of *Ellen Middleton*, Lady Georgiana Fullerton. Lady Georgiana was the daughter of the first Earl Granville and a granddaughter of the fifth Duke of Devonshire. She had spent her youth in Paris where her father was British Ambassador, and it was there she married Mr. Fullerton and started her career as a religious novelist. Both she and her husband were converts from Anglicanism. To their great grief their only son died at the age of twenty-one and from then on neither of them ever put off their mourning. To the end of her life Lady Georgiana dressed in the poorest clothes, ate the simplest food, gave away all her money to charitable causes and founded a religious order to work amongst the destitute.

Such were the people Maria found herself among. Madame was delighted. A Protestant herself, she was both too civilized and too erratic to commit her mind firmly to any one ecclesiastical position. She did not dislike Catholics, especially when they behaved as if they were aristocratic members of the Salvation Army. She encouraged Maria in her new friendships and urged her to stay with the Comptons for as long as she pleased.

It chanced that Maria was asked by Lady Georgiana to help one afternoon with a tea party for the poor children of the parish of the Sacred Heart. Pauline von Hügel sent the carriage to Dr. Compton's house and they set off together. Lady Georgiana instructed them to pour out the lemonade and to see that the children had a wholesome slice of bread and butter before they moved on to the cake. Maria did as she was told, but before long her attention was struck by the sight of an exceptionally good looking man with black curly hair and blue eyes who was sitting astride a chair and stuffing a child at the table with custard trifle.

She asked Pauline who he was. 'A Mr. Shepheard,' she replied. 'Mr. Shepheard, from Norfolk. We hope,' she added in a lower tone, 'that he will be received into the Church before so very long.'

Maria walked towards him and laughingly took the plate out of his hands.

'At this rate you'll make the child sick,' she said.

Maria Pasqua at the time of her marriage

Maria Pasqua in 1879,
aged twenty-three

Philip Shepheard in
1883

SIX

In the same year that Domenico sold Maria Pasqua to Madame de Noailles, a young Norfolk doctor started work in his first practice. His name was Philip Candler Shepheard, the eleventh and last surviving child of John Shepheard who lived at Erpingham, a small place about twelve miles north of Norwich.

The Shepheards were Norfolk people, born and bred. They came originally from the coast where they had for generations farmed by the edge of the encroaching sea at Happisburgh and Bacton, building their substantial houses from flints carted from the old Priory. Philip's mother was Charlotte Marsh, one of the daughters of the local rector, who in his youth had translated Juvenal and one fine October day in 1794 had played whist and eaten his way through an enormous dinner given by Parson Woodforde. 'A sensible young man,' the diarist remarked, 'and a clergyman.' In 1840, when Philip was only two years old, Charlotte died giving birth to a twelfth child.

Although his eldest daughter was seventeen at the time of his wife's death and able to help to look after the younger members of the family, John Shepheard was responsible for eleven motherless children and had six sons to provide for. Before the extension of the railways it was not usual for the provincial middle classes to send their sons to public schools. They attended the local grammar school and were later apprenticed to some profession or sent to sea. Some went to the university in the hope of obtaining a curacy. Philip lived as a boarder in the home of the village schoolmaster at a little hamlet called Roughton on the flat heathlands between Norwich and Cromer. He had lessons with the other pupils and was given extra coaching by the master who lived in the schoolhouse with his mother, an old lady who took snuff from a tortoiseshell box.

If his education was old-fashioned it was nothing like so narrowly classical as that of most of his contemporaries. At the schoolmaster's house he learnt mathematics, geography, and natural history. In the evening they would read together essays from the *Spectator* and the *Rambler*, the letters of Lord Chesterfield, the poems of Hood and of Gray. Philip did not lack companions and, free from the tyranny of compulsory games, was able to roam the countryside as he pleased.

At home in the holidays he was cared for by his sisters, and his father and brothers taught him to shoot, fish and ride. Once when he was about ten his father took him to a shoot at Lord Suffield's. It happened that the Duke of Wellington was there, an old man then and slow on his feet. Passing by an oak tree the Duke bent down with a grunt and picked up an unusually large acorn. He stood looking at it as it lay in the palm of his hand then beckoned to Philip. 'My boy,' he said, 'plant this when you get home. Give it plenty of room. You may depend upon it, it will please your posterity.' This oak still stands today, a fine tree in the grounds of Erpingham House.

It was fortunate for John Shepheard's children that their mother's brother, Major Marsh, was a bachelor. As a young man Major Marsh had fought and had been wounded while serving under Wellington in the Peninsular War. He had been very fond of his sister Charlotte and on his retirement lived at Erpingham and did everything he could to help her children. He paid for his eldest nephew, Sam, to go to his grandfather's college at Cambridge, and for another nephew to train as a physician. Medicine seemed to run in the family. Charlotte's younger sister, Anna Cooper, had a son called Alfred, born in the same year as Philip, who was studying to be a doctor. Influenced by his first cousin and his brother, Philip decided that with the Major's help he would follow in their footsteps.

He left Norfolk for the first time in his life for St. Thomas's Hospital in London. He had very little money and worked hard, coming home only in the summer. He passed his final exams successfully, doing so well in surgery that it was suggested he might copy his cousin Alfred and specialize in it. Philip, however, disliked the idea of being poor and dependent for another five years. Instead he went as houseman to various hospitals but resented being cooped up in industrial towns.

Restless, filled with undirected ambition, he chafed against his narrow circumstances and set out on a visit to Canada, hoping that he might find more scope there for the kind of life he wanted to lead.

He found nothing that suited him and on his return home the old Major once more came to his rescue. He said he would help to set him up in practice. Philip answered an advertisement from an elderly doctor seeking a partner at a small place called Gayton, not far from King's Lynn, in west Norfolk. There was excellent shooting there and far better hunting than on the other side of the county. The old doctor liked him and offered him a partnership with the right of succession.

Philip was now twenty-seven. He was unusually handsome in a dark Byronic manner, with black curly hair and blue eyes. He took lodgings in a house off the old coach road between Lynn and Norwich and made his rounds on horseback. He was a good doctor with a quiet confident manner, and soon became popular in the district.

He had been at Gayton for a little over a year when he had a call from the owner of a house on the outskirts of the village.

A certain Miss Ellen Simson sent her groom to ask if Dr. Shepheard would kindly call at Bridge House and see one of her maids who was running a high temperature. Philip examined the girl and then asked to speak to her mistress. He was shown into the drawing-room.

Ellen was the only surviving child of Alexander Simson, a mahogany merchant, of Highbury Park, London. He had died some time ago, her mother the previous year. She lived on her own in her father's country house with a housekeeper and servants. Although the Simsons were not Philip's patients, he had seen Ellen in church and about the village: at that time she was somewhere in her early fifties, rather stout, with hair dragged back from her face into a heavy net. He stood by the door and spoke in his habitual quiet, rather curt, manner. The maidservant was suffering from scarlet fever. It was rampant in the village. The vicarage children were down with it. He had given the girl some powders to lower her temperature and would return tomorrow. Ellen was grateful. She had promised the girl's mother to act as a second parent. If Dr. Shepheard were to call the next morning she would be able to tell him what sort of night the child had spent.

Bridge House is still there, the drawing-room where Philip and Ellen met still exists, but nothing more now can ever be known of their courtship. Which one it was who edged forward first, who hinted at a closer relationship and smoothed away the apparently insuperable difficulties, can only be conjectured. Eighteen months later, early in the morning of 23 September 1869, they were married at Gayton church.

It cannot be supposed that Philip was in love with his wife or that he would have married her if she had not been rich. But the marriage was a happy one and he was attentive and loyal. However unprepossessing Ellen's appearance might have been, she was a woman of wide interests, a good musician, a fearless rider to hounds and an amusing talker. She adored her husband, gave him everything she had in the world, and was fearful only that people would mock at their disparity of age or that such a handsome man would fall victim to the wiles of a younger woman. She had no need for anxiety. Infidelity was not in Philip's nature.

He gave up his profession completely. From the moment he led his bride down the aisle of Gayton church, past the two stained glass windows presented by her father and out into the autumn sunshine, the only people he ever treated again were his tenants.

Their wedding journey lasted five weeks and was spent in London and the West Country. They visited Exeter, Lynmouth, Lynton and Ilfracombe. Ellen saw the house where Shelley had stayed, took a trip in a fishing boat and picked sprigs of heather to pin in her album. Before they returned she suggested that Philip might not wish to go on living at Gayton, but he was not a man to care about gossip, least of all to be intimidated by it. He liked the house, he liked the hunting: in any case they intended to spend part of the year travelling.

Together they toured Scotland, Wales, and the Lakes, went to the Derby, to Ascot and to Henley, to concerts in London. Ellen pressed wild flowers from Wordsworth's grave, grasses from Coleridge's and practised on her Collard and Collard. Philip fished, hunted, had his sisters over to stay, heard his brother Sam preach at Calthorpe and dined at Lord Orford's. In 1873, the good old Major died at Erpingham; and one evening in the summer of the following year Ellen asked Philip's advice. She was frightened, she said. For some time now she had felt lumps on her breast. She desperately wanted reassurance and would like him to examine her.

Philip took her to London to consult a surgeon who confirmed his fears. It was too late to operate. They returned to Gayton and six months later, in the early January of 1875, Ellen died and was buried by the may tree in the far corner of the bracken covered churchyard at Ashwicken. Her pain and her unexpected happiness were at an end. Exhausted by the anguish of the past weeks, Philip left Norfolk for Switzerland.

SEVEN

As a widower Philip found himself more closely involved with the concerns of his family and influenced by decisions which some of them had most painfully arrived at.

It had all started long ago when they were young together at Erpingham House. In those days, when Philip himself was still a child living with the schoolmaster at Roughton, only his sisters Mary, Charlotte, and Susanna were out of the schoolroom. Their father, John Shepheard, was conscious that he had five daughters to settle in life and was tolerably pleased when he heard that a certain John Mack of Paston Hall was not merely looking out for a wife but casting his eyes in the direction of his girls at Erpingham. They were less gratified. John Mack may have been rich and master of the white square house in its plantations at Paston, but he was forty-five and had the reputation of being ill-tempered. Mary was told to invite him over.

In the country at that time the ritual of taking people into dinner was far less rigid than it afterwards became, and therefore capable of variations which were well understood by everyone present. John Mack arrived. At first he talked easily enough to their father and to their brother, Sam, just down from Cambridge, but then fell silent. His eyes wandered from one girl to the next, appraising, evaluating, pondering. The dinner gong sounded. John Mack rose when Mary did, but it was to Susanna that he gave his arm.

She was only eighteen, but she married him and bore him

eleven children. As time went on and he became more sullen and set in his ways she felt a mischievous urge to annoy him. She decided to play upon his notorious dislike of the Church of Rome.

John Mack was not a stupid man, but his understanding was limited and he knew very little indeed about the religion of his forebears. He was patron of the living at Paston; every Sunday he and his household went through the private gate and took the path which led from the Hall through the churchyard and into the squire's pew. He did not in any way connect his beautiful church with the Catholic liturgy for which it had been built. He had neither read nor attended a Mass; it was for him an unformulated threat, a vague and foreign spectre, Catholicism itself an unpleasant interlude in the history of respectable religion.

Determined to vex him, Susanna bought books by the distinguished converts Manning and Newman, together with devotional works by Faber and controversial Catholic pamphlets. These she scattered about the house, in her husband's study, by his bed, at the side of his favourite armchair. He remained impervious but she was trapped by her own bait.

As she read, it seemed to her that she had spent much of her life straining at gnats and swallowing camels. If, which she did not doubt, by words and water anyone could cleanse a baby from original sin and snatch him from eternal damnation, it was nothing so extraordinary for a priest to have the power to absolve sin and to make Christ truly present for our worship on the altar.

Where was the logic of it all? If one thought that the early Councils of the Church taught the truth, why not the later? By what authority had Luther and Calvin so priggishly set themselves above the living religion of over a thousand years? She sat under the thatched roof in the gloom of her mutilated church and wondered at the parched holy-water stoups, the empty niches, the desolate altar and the sad slabs of the sedilia.

Like most of her family, her mind was sharp but not specu-
lative. The central anguish of the age to which Newman really
addressed himself did not bother her. She did not feel that the
truths of the spirit were attached to impossible propositions.
She accepted the existence of God and the Christian revelation
without question. What she doubted was the Protestant
understanding of it.

Thoroughly punished for her treatment of her husband,
Susanna became anxious and perplexed and continually asked
herself what in fact really had happened at the Reformation.
Had her family been brought up in a religion which was a
radically impoverished version of the faith it supplanted? What
would Philip say to this, what would her brother Sam, the
cheerful Vicar of Calthorpe, think about it all? Did he really
believe that he was a priest of the universal Church, ordained in
the Apostolic Succession, a living part of that vast communion
of souls on earth, in purgatory, and in heaven of which her
books spoke so eloquently?

The Vicar of Calthorpe thought no such thing because he
had never even considered the matter. Sam was a typical
eighteenth-century clergyman in the old low church tradition.
He baptized, visited the sick, and every Sunday his rural
congregation watched the sand trickle through the pulpit
hourglass as he read his grandfather's sermons.

He was squire as well as parson, farming his own land and
understanding his people's problems. He thought there was
nothing unseemly in conducting morning prayer wearing his
hunting stock, in announcing the latest prices at Norwich
market from the chancel steps or having a joke at the expense
of his parishioners. Once he put up a notice on the door which
read, 'church closed because of family bereavement'. His
favourite cow had died.

His church was his own, an extension of his personality, as
much a meeting place for the village as a place of worship. He

loved to tell the story of the farmer who before the service
begged him to ask the congregation whether anyone had seen
a sow of his which had disappeared. The farmer was deaf and,
during the pause that followed Sam's announcement of the
banns of a projected marriage, shouted in a loud voice from the
back of the church, 'and if she's got a great big wart on the
middle of her back, she's mine'.

It so happened that Sam's neighbour, Lord Orford, was a
Catholic convert and an ardent Jacobite. An eccentric man, he
treated his vicar with affectionate mockery, and used to produce him at dinner at Mannington Hall as an extinct species, a
bucolic clergyman of the old school, a curious survival of the
hard-drinking, Latin-quoting, hunting parson of the previous
century.

Lord Orford was a compulsive womanizer who fathered a
whole brood of illegitimate children in the district and insisted
that if they were boys each one should be called Horatio
Walpole. This did not make for domestic peace. One day his
wife lost patience and tied a piece of string across the turret
stair at Mannington Hall. Not seeing it in the gloom, her
husband's latest mistress fell down the stairs and broke her hip.
Orford was furious with his wife, there was an appalling scene
and he rode over to Sam for consolation.

In afterdays Sam would point with his stick to the very spot
where their conversation had taken place. Together they rode
up and down, Orford as usual complaining, expostulating and
protesting about the wretchedness of all women. Suddenly he
reined in his horse at a gate and fell silent. Then he turned to
Sam and announced that he had known all along that what had
happened was a judgement of God. He had lived for years in
mortal sin, he must now repent, go to confession, receive
absolution and with the help of the sacraments live a better life
in future.

Sam was thunderstruck. He knew Lord Orford was a

Catholic but he had never heard an Englishman refer to confession before. Clergyman as he himself was, he had never indeed spoken seriously to his friend about religion or imagined that a gentleman ever did. Slowly he returned to Erpingham House, ruminating on what had occurred, only to find Susanna waiting for him.

The Shepheard family were split down the middle, half remaining where they were, half becoming Catholics. Susanna and two of her sisters were the first to be received. After a struggle, Sam resigned the living of Calthorpe and joined them. But Philip was extremely cautious by nature. He determined to sift the matter thoroughly, and was the last to come in.

It was not a thing lightly done. Unlike many converts, none of the Shepheards were extravagant in the exercise of their faith or contemptuous of their Protestant past, which they looked upon not as wrong but incomplete. But it was hard for them to be separated from the grey flint churches of their youth, never again to attend services at Calthorpe and Lamas, or to worship at Erpingham where their parents lay under the table tomb by the west door.

Ellen had been dead for over a year and Philip not yet received into the Church when his sister Charlotte suggested one day that it might do him good to go for a month or two to Bournemouth. He agreed, settled at Stewart's Hotel and introduced himself to the local Catholic priest. Soon he met the old Baroness von Hügel and her daughter Pauline, and before long Lady Georgiana Fullerton engaged his services to help with a party for the poor children.

He was willing enough and was sitting in the church hall rather absent-mindedly spooning trifle into a child's mouth when he found the plate lifted very gently out of his hands. Glancing up he observed a slight girl with wavy brown hair and the most beautiful eyes he had ever seen.

'At this rate,' she said, 'you'll make the child sick.'

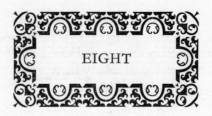

EIGHT

Philip was attracted to Maria Pasqua the moment he saw her. Reserved and silent himself, always slow to give an opinion, he was fascinated by her vivacity, her quick replies, the ardour of a nature so different from his own. He took care to cultivate the von Hügels and to make himself useful to Lady Georgiana, and by these means found ample opportunity to meet Maria. With a precipitancy unlike his usual extreme caution, within a few weeks he made up his mind to marry her. The fact that she was Italian he did not consider to be a serious drawback. Her early adventures, although they ought not to be dwelt upon, added to her piquancy. At thirty-eight he was still in the prime of his life, comfortably off and ready to provide a home for her. He did not anticipate any serious difficulties. In this he was mistaken. Once it had been Ellen who had loved and suffered, now it was Philip's turn. It took over four years of persistent wooing to make Maria his wife.

It was his unexpected likeness to Domenico which had made her so impulsively cross the room and speak to Philip, but when Maria saw how much she attracted him and learnt that he had extended his stay in Bournemouth, she took fright and made an excuse to return home. She was only twenty-one and had no experience whatsoever of the world outside the closed circle of Madame and her friends, nor any roots to anchor her from the wind. She was frightened of life in general, of men in particular, she did not know quite what she wanted or the kind of person she really was.

At her departure, Philip left for Norfolk. He spent some of the winter hunting and shooting at Gayton and set out for Davos in the New Year of 1878. Before he left he sent Christmas greetings to the von Hügels and the Comptons, assuring them that he would see them all again in the summer after the Ascot races.

He did as he had promised, first of all calling upon the old Baroness to inquire whether Maria Pasqua was staying with Dr. and Mrs. Compton. Hearing that this was so, he made his way to Christchurch and sent in his card. He found Maria and Mrs. Compton in the morning-room making raffia table napkin rings. He looked at Maria to see if she was well, then somewhat brusquely asked Mrs. Compton if she thought that he ought to call upon Madame de Noailles before paying his renewed respects to Miss Abruzzesi.

Maria was dismayed. She had thought about Philip a great deal that winter, wondering when exactly he would come again and what she would say to him when he did, but it had never entered her head that he would ask to see Madame. Once he went to Eastbourne she would be immediately recalled to Holywell Lodge and imprisoned there with Miss Roche and the dogs for the rest of the summer.

She remained silent, and it was left for Mrs. Compton to say that there was no necessity to call upon Madame de Noailles. Maria was under Dr. Compton's protection, and as a friend of the Baroness it was quite in order for Mr. Shepheard to visit their house if he wished.

Philip took Maria for a walk along the cliffs to Boscombe Chine. It was the first time she had ever been alone with a man. He spoke about his family, his sister Susanna from Paston and Charlotte and Betty who looked after his brother Sam at Erpingham House. She thought the name Erpingham a strange one and it gave her an unpleasant jolt to hear that Sam was nearly sixty.

He told her about his home at Gayton, Mrs. Woods his housekeeper, and how in Norfolk the fields stretched to the horizon. She said that she had never visited Norfolk but when they crossed from Harwich to the Hook Madame often re-marked how similar the Dutch landscape was. Philip stopped, with his back to the sea. It was such rich soil, he said, moving his finger and thumb as if to test the grain, amongst the most fertile in England. She shivered, already feeling the cutting wind blowing over mile after mile of desolate stubble. Yet even while shivering she thought she loved him, that he looked very well with his ruffled hair and fine hands.

Before Philip left for home and his winter travels he bought Maria a coral necklace. He remembered, he said, her telling him how much her own people loved corals. She accepted it, still not knowing what she felt or how to explain this to him.

That winter Philip was received into the Church, and when he was in Switzerland he took daily lessons to improve his French conversation. On his return he found Maria rather distant. It was an excellent thing, of course, for him to become a Catholic, and to be able to talk French was always an advant-age. It could not, however, affect her in any way. Not affect her in any way? What could she mean? He could not make pretty speeches like some men but surely she knew how beautiful he thought her and how sincerely he wished her to be his wife? She had accepted the necklace and given him reason to suppose that she cared. Maria remained confused and silent, quite unable to tell him to his face that for reasons she was not clear about herself, she could come to no decision. Eventually Philip told her that perhaps it would be better for them both if he spent the rest of the Season in London and then went abroad as usual. When he returned he would expect an answer.

Maria had no one to advise her. The only women she knew at all intimately were Madame de Noailles and Miss Roche. Madame was useless, Miss Roche an inexperienced elderly spinster. Pauline von Hügel was her own age and understood the world, but had rejected it and considered herself now only as the Bride of Christ. Lady Georgiana was of a different generation, and although in her novels she seemed to understand all sorts of emotional situations, in real life she was totally absorbed in the collection of woollen vests for the orphans of the diocese. Such people lived in a rarefied atmosphere – she herself could not breathe it all the time without hypocrisy. She loved God, she hoped she did, she would always do what was right, but she could not exist on their plane, giving up everything, thinking all the time about prayer and poor children.

She wanted to enjoy herself, to see life, to talk and to dance and to laugh, not to be imprisoned, controlled, compelled to be good. She was getting old, twenty-three, twenty-four, twenty-five, thirty, she would soon be middle-aged and if Madame died who would look after her? Would she have to live alone with Miss Roche? If Philip had taken Ellen to Ascot he could take her too. They could stay in London and go to the theatre, they might even travel to Italy together before they settled down at Gayton. She did not doubt that Philip was a kind and good man. What she questioned was the quality of her love, the purity of her motives, the wisdom of marrying someone whose temperament and interests were so different from her own.

She received a laconic letter from Scotland and another from Paris, and before she went back to Eastbourne Mrs. Compton told her that she had had a talk with the Doctor and they both felt it was time for Maria to speak to Madame de Noailles. Besides, Mr. Shepheard was bound to continue to correspond from abroad, and it was not right to go on concealing letters with foreign stamps.

Madame did not fly into a rage but sat in silence for so long that Miss Roche thought that she had had a stroke. It was rather sly of the Comptons. If they had been more explicit about Mr. Shepheard before this she would speedily have put an end to the friendship. She would not go so far as to accuse Maria of a clandestine relationship, but she had imagined from her conversation and from what others had told her that Mr. Shepheard was merely a middle-aged widower good enough to interest himself in charitable projects.

A man who had once been a general practitioner was hardly a suitable match. She had never heard of anyone bearing that name being received in Norfolk. What had been the profession of his father? A farmer, did Maria say? A *gentleman* farmer, Maria pointed out. His grandfather had been the local rector and besides that, Lord of the Manor of Lamas. Madame sniffed and said that she thought the Lubbocks had the Manor of Lamas. What sort of house did she intend going to? Well, eight acres and six principal bedrooms sounded respectable provided the building was nowhere near stagnant water. But how did Maria think she could manage without her? Miss Roche could not live for ever. Who would read to her then? Was not Maria a trifle lukewarm? Did she wish to get married or did she not? She must take it from her that all men, without exception, were thoroughly selfish and if Maria had any regard for her own interests, not to speak of other people's, she would remain where she was.

Letters came regularly from Davos and, towards the end of the year, from Basle. Madame complained of a cold in her eyes, and told Miss Roche to write a letter to Philip to await his arrival in Norfolk and invite him to Holywell Lodge. Maria thought that if Philip put off coming to Eastbourne until the spring it would mean that he did not really care for her any more. If he came that winter then he still loved her as much as ever and if she did not say she would marry him at once, she would agree definitely to do so one day.

The afternoon he arrived Madame was in bed with a bad throat. Maria heard the wheels of the station fly on the gravel and called Miss Roche. It was sleeting slightly and Miss Roche rubbed the misted pane of the drawing-room window with the side of her fist so that she could see better.

Conversation at tea was easy enough. Philip said little about his travels, his mind seemed rather to collect itself round Norfolk and the places he loved. They had read in the papers about that fellow Parnell and his campaign in Ireland to isolate anyone taking over a farm from an evicted tenant? Well, when he was still at school at Roughton he went about with a boy a good deal older than himself who liked climbing church towers. One morning both of them scrambled up the stairway at Hanworth, right to the top, like Pasqua's mountain, and dared each other to swing round the flagstaff, feet over the parapet. He did it first but when his companion's turn came there was a terrible crack and the flagstaff splintered right through. Luckily he was able to seize his friend by the knees and drag him down on to the leads. If he had not done so Parnell and his lot would have been cheated out of their first victim and, come to that, all of them out of a new word. His friend's name was Charles Boycott.

Philip told his tale with a modesty and clarity which impressed Miss Roche. She thought his dark curls and blue eyes romantic and began to envy Maria, to regret her own life, to wonder how long it would be before Madame died and she herself could be independent.

Almost as soon as Philip had met Maria, Madame de Noailles's influence had made itself felt. He was irritated by the power she exerted, although conscious of the folly of alienating her. However, he was not a man to be frightened of anyone; on the contrary, he was glad at last to have an opportunity of speaking to her. The first thing he noticed when he entered her bedroom next morning was the strange effect produced by the replacement of half the window panes with red glass. Madame had this done in all her houses. She was convinced that it produced a cheerful outlook and was good for the health.

The sleet had turned to rain which trickled down the window pane like thin drops of blood. Madame was a most extraordinary sight. She lay propped up on pillows in the sunset glow of her four poster bed, round her forehead a stocking filled with grey squirrel's fur, another wrapped about her chin. The end of the stocking trailed over one eye, causing her to squint like an elderly pirate. She trusted he would forgive her for receiving him in bed, but she understood he was not unaccustomed to it.

Philip was imperturbable and Madame, while continuing to insist upon the wickedness of Maria making any sort of marriage, had to confess that she found nothing against him personally. Only Maria must make up her mind: there was nothing so ill bred as to keep a man dangling.

Maria had in fact made up her mind and was very happy. She would marry Philip, not this year, but the next. She knew now that everything was going to be all right. It was not until Philip began to press her for a definite date that she began once more to feel uneasy, an uneasiness that as the days passed grew into panic. Like some creature once trapped and now compelled to drag its leg, she had a deep fear of being finally caught. She was torn between her love for Philip, delight at being loved, and terror of committing herself beyond recall.

Back in Bournemouth, she consulted Mrs. Compton. Mrs. Compton had long thought that the life Maria Pasqua led was unnatural, that Madame de Noailles was not fitted to bring up a girl, and that Philip would make a devoted and steady husband. She shrank, however, from the responsibility of urging anyone to marry a man she herself was doubtful of being happy with. Maria was left to make her own decision.

She wrote to Philip to say that she realized now that the whole thing had been a mistake. They differed too greatly in their interests and temperament. She had indeed loved him when she had said she did, but never in the way he loved her.

She hoped that he would forgive her and find a wife more suited to him than she could ever be.

As soon as she had posted the letter she felt tremendous relief, a guilty surge of joy. She was free again, free to meet anybody or nobody, free to die an old maid or to marry a millionaire, to become a nun or trim hats in Paris. A few days later she went for a walk in the meadows by the ruins of Christchurch Priory. It was a beautiful afternoon in late May and she sat on the grass watching an ant climb slowly up a daisy stalk and a pollen-laden bumblebee shuffle along the little path she had made for it with her fingers. Her relief from anxiety, her narrow escape, made her feel close to all living things, each one, like her, so intent on life but at the mercy of a foot or a finger nail. She looked up and the world that a moment ago had stretched before her in such infinite variety contracted into a single black-coated figure.

Philip had been shocked to receive her letter and had left Norfolk by the first train to find her. It was only a fit of nerves, he said, quite natural. Most girls felt like that before they left home. Of course they were suited to each other, of course they would be happy together, as they always had been. He had a beautiful home all ready for her, she must come and share it with him. Once they were married everything would come all right. Never mind that Madame had been told that the engagement was broken off. This time he would announce it in the newspapers and write to her that very day.

So it was done, and Madame's response was brief and enigmatic.

Dear Mr. Shepheard,

I am very glad of yr explanation of the announcement of yr engagement, for I know Maria has always been deeply attached to you and I, in common with others, believe her nature to be a *rara avis* in creation. I therefore rejoice at the conclusion of this painful business with all my heart! I will ask Dr. Compton to write to you re the arrangements between us and, hoping to renew yr acquaintance ere long,

I remain,

Yours truly,

H. de Noailles

If she could not bring herself to attend the wedding, Madame provided a generous dowry. On the day Maria wore a dress of cream silk edged with orange embroidery.

The ceremony took place on 17 August 1881, in the church of Our Lady, Star of the Sea, Eastbourne. Maria was twenty-five, Philip was forty-two. Dr. Compton gave her away, Miss Roche was witness. Domenico was prevented from undertaking his natural duty, but he would have been delighted to have seen himself described on their marriage certificate as a gentleman.

The honeymoon was spent at Tunbridge Wells where Lady Georgiana, happening to be there on diocesan business, caught sight of Maria's bright face at Mass and wrote to wish her joy. Maria was happy. She was looking forward to her new home and although she did not know it, had already conceived her first child.

NINE

Little marred Philip Shepheard's happiness on their journey into Norfolk save some admiring glances cast at his wife from a man wearing lavender coloured gloves, who happened to share their compartment in the train to King's Lynn. He was taking the woman he had loved for so long to a place he considered to be in every way a perfect home.

The carriage met them at the station and they drove the six miles to Gayton past the still and dusty hedgerows of late summer. Bridge House was separated from the road only by a row of tall trees and a small circular drive. The time of the train's arrival was known, the distance nicely calculated, and hardly had the carriage wheels crunched the gravel before the front door opened. The first to emerge was Philip's sister Charlotte, then came her sister Betty, followed by the housekeeper, Mrs. Woods, Fanny Bell the housemaid, the cook, the kitchen maid and the outdoor servants.

Charlotte was fifty-six, gaunt, with a prominent nose, Betty twelve years younger. Neither of them was pleased by Philip's marriage. Charlotte had been a second mother to him, Betty his playmate; both had hoped that as a widower he would come and live with Sam and themselves at Erpingham. They had been very fond of Ellen and understood her. They heartily disliked foreigners, had no desire to go abroad, did not speak French, nor approve of artists. When Philip had first told them that he was engaged to an Italian they thought he was joking. Downright to the point of rudeness, they mistook Maria's desire to please for insincerity. Although kind-hearted and good people, they never succeeded in crossing the gulf or dissolving the antagonism latent in that first encounter.

They shook hands, the servants curtsied, Charlotte gave directions about the disposition of the luggage and Betty took Maria Pasqua upstairs to take off her hat and coat. She stood, lonely and rather frightened, before the oval glass with its neat hair tidies on the tall mahogany dressing table. Ellen's silver brushes and long-handled mirror lay there patiently waiting and in front of them someone had pricked out 'Welcome the Bride' onto a red plush pincushion.

Marriage was not as Maria Pasqua imagined it. Mrs. Woods was determined to keep the running of the household in her own hands and she wished everything to be done in exactly the same way as it had been when Ellen was alive. She was used to ordering the house without interference, to long lazy months when Philip was abroad or in London. For her the good days were over. She resented her new mistress and barely concealed her contempt for her inexperience. Maria did not know how to deal with her. She lacked both the courage and hardness of heart to ask for her dismissal, nor was she certain that she would be able to manage without her. She did not feel yet ready to give orders directly to Cook, or grasp the lines of demarcation between Fanny Bell and the young parlourmaid just imported from the village. Madame de Noailles had taught her manners, had seen that she appreciated books and pictures, enjoyed history and tales about curious places, but she had told her no more about the ordinary running of a household than she had about the intimacies of married life. It was useless to appeal to Philip: for him Mrs. Woods was the lynch-pin of his establishment, someone who had been devoted to Ellen, who knew exactly how he liked things to be done and had kept the home going through the difficult years of his early widowhood. Pasqua was lucky to have her.

The countryside round Gayton is not perhaps the most attractive in Norfolk. The village is remote, low-lying and sprawls along a flat and damp plain. When September came Philip spent a great deal of time shooting and Maria was left with little to do. Madame wrote to warn her that the cold weather was approaching. Did she remember the happy days they had spent together in Burgundy and how in winter there the sheep had to be protected by stone walls? Surely they would all be frozen to death at Gayton?

A few people in the district called, mostly out of curiosity, and Maria found them as dull as they thought her strange. Rumours had preceded her arrival; some had heard that she was the natural daughter of an earl, a few were certain that her father had been an Italian count ennobled by the Pope for defending Rome against Garibaldi. Maria returned the calls punctiliously and left the correct number of cards, but she was disappointed that most of the conversation was about shooting, servants or the weather. No one talked about Wilkie Collins or the ideas of William Morris, and none of them seemed even to have heard of Coventry Patmore.

Susanna came over to stay. Long widowed, complaining and plump, wearing a small medallion engraved with a skull and cross bones on a velvet ribbon round her neck, she had resigned Paston Hall to one of her sons and his pretty wife. The girl was hopelessly extravagant, she told Philip, and spent far too much on entertaining. But if she was blunt, Susanna was also kind, and something in Maria's wistful expression touched her. Young people would be young people, she said. They should drive over to Paston and stay for one of Nellie's parties.

Nothing could have been further from Philip's mind. By now he was hunting three days a week. Maria did not ride. As a child she had been frightened even of ponies, and Madame, constantly on the move, had never found an opportunity to rid her of her fear or time for instruction. With very little to occupy her, Maria ordered the carriage and drove along the country lanes by herself. More often, she sat alone in the drawing-room and brooded over another woman's possessions.

She hated to think that Philip had been married before and above all to someone so plain. She put away one framed photograph and even removed some likenesses of Ellen from their scalloped windows in the Simson album. Then, con-science-stricken, as if she were defrauding some future genera-tion of a truth it had a right to know, she found two small oval pictures and folded them together in a piece of paper. On the outside she wrote in her round, generous hand, 'Ellen Simson and Philip Candler Shepheard, 1869. At the time of their marriage'.

The trees outside the drawing-room window had been planted too near the house and on particularly gloomy days she transcribed sad verses from Lamartine into her commonplace book or tried to read French romances sent to her from the rue Garancière in Paris. She began to lament her friends in Bourne-mouth and to miss Madame and even Miss Roche. Everything in the house, from a new riding habit gathering dust in an empty bedroom to half-used reels of cotton in her work-box, remained as Ellen had left it. In the drawing-room her piano stood with its music stacked into a neat pile, on the tapestry stool her marbled covered scrapbooks and in the drawer of her writing desk slim volumes of her diaries. Three notebooks covered the five years of her married life.

Fearful that Mrs. Woods might come in, Maria opened the glossy black covers and pondered deeply over the entries, each one meticulously written with a fine pencil in a sloping hand. So the sun had shone on their wedding day and for his first Christmas present Philip had given her a signet ring. She knew old Simson's crest as well as she knew the chimes of the clock he had given to the village church – it was on the candlesticks, the silver and the fat clumsy seals from his watch chain she had seen in Philip's study.

Morbid curiosity led her to concentrate on the last notebook, where the pencil jottings were fewer and more difficult to read. Ellen had been taken in a wheel chair into the garden. She felt very poorly. Philip was hunting. Philip was shooting. Philip was at the market in Lynn. So that's how it was. People die and life goes on all the same. The Vicar came to give Ellen the Sacrament. She could no longer get downstairs. Two months before her death, the entries ceased altogether.

Had she been buried wearing the signet ring? Where in fact had she been buried? She could not ask Philip. Was Ellen so very much older than he was? Was that why the page recording her birth had been torn out of the Simson family Bible? Was her age on her gravestone? Should she ask Mrs. Woods, quite casually, where the funeral had taken place? The outrageousness of such an inquiry made her want to laugh and then she cried. She was determined not to give birth to her child in the bed in which Ellen had died and when Philip came back to luncheon she would tell him so.

He made no comment other than to suggest that they should take Madame de Noailles's advice and go abroad for the rest of the winter. Maria was overjoyed. They could go to Italy and stay in Rome. She would cross the Alps again and into the sunlit plains of Lombardy. She would return to Velletri and find Domenico and her brothers. Philip privately thought Domenico a scoundrel. He refused. Madame would be extremely displeased. Maria answered that she did not belong to Madame any more. She belonged to herself. In any case, Philip pointed out, even if such a meeting could be arranged, it would turn out to be an embarrassment for both sides. She would quickly discover that they no longer had anything in common.

Maria was convinced that she had more in common with her own people than she had with her husband's. She imagined

Domenico, more lined now and with his black hair grizzled at the temples, clasping her in his arms and assuring her that he had handed her over to Madame de Noailles solely for her own good, while her three brothers, grown tall and handsome, stood by his side and removed their hats in admiration at their sister's beauty and fine clothes.

They set out for Davos in the late autumn. Philip preferred to go to a place he knew, so they stayed at the same hotel he had frequented before their marriage. Maria enjoyed the journey to Switzerland but when she got there she found that her life was as constricted as ever. Philip had ordered a sitting-room for their private use and she spent her time either there or walking alone with him. She met her fellow guests only at meals: talking and laughter were for ever in the next room, at the next table, on another staircase. Philip wished to meet nobody and could not understand that she might want to. He desired no introductions and repelled all overtures. He had abandoned his customary employments to come to Davos for her sake since Bridge House so inexplicably had inflamed her nerves, and he wanted no other society. She must surely feel the same way. But she could not. She loved him, but she could not.

So she sat in their room and crocheted and sewed endless garments for the baby, torn between boredom and dread of returning to Gayton. She told Philip that when she got home and after the child was born, she intended to write something. She had so much in her head, ideas leaping like lambs, thoughts as swift as sunbeams. He smiled at her fancy and told her the baby would take up far more of her time than she imagined. He wished to return in March but she would not. So desolate an image of Bridge House was impressed upon her mind that she did not believe him when he told her the daffodils would be out and the apple blossom, that the swallows would soon be nesting in the coach house eaves. It would be unpleasant to have the child born on foreign soil and further delay would make it too late for her to travel.

They returned to Gayton a week before the arrival of the monthly nurse whom Madame had sent on Lady Georgiana's recommendation. The baby was born on Tuesday, 23 May 1882. Outside the house the peonies were in full bloom. It was market day and Philip had to be recalled from Lynn.

The child was a girl, long and thin, the image, Philip said, of his sister Charlotte. The monthly nurse, who had made great friends with Mrs. Woods, declared that first babies were always delicate and it was unlikely that this one would live. Maria was determined that she should and, although she had a breast abscess, fed her herself. Her tears mingled with her milk and the nurse implored her to put the infant on a bottle. Maria persevered, eventually the baby thrived and was taken to King's Lynn to be baptized in the beautiful christening robes made for her by Lady Webster of Battle Abbey. She was called Helena, after her godmother Madame de Noailles, who wrote at once to say that on no account should the child be vaccinated. She had read in a medical journal that the lymph used had been proved to contain cancer microbes.

TEN

They did not stay long at Gayton. Maria Pasqua knew that Ellen was the real mistress of the house and that she herself lacked the strength of character to impose her will upon a ghost. So she ordered meals that Ellen would have eaten, kept to the domestic timetable Ellen had decreed, saw to it that everything down to the soap the servants used in their bedrooms was exactly the same as it had been in Ellen's life. Her actions, however, were prompted by something deeper than fear of displeasing Mrs. Woods. She was alive and Ellen was dead, she had a child and Ellen was barren. She could not so much as move a piece of furniture without feeling that she was taking an unfair advantage, injuring a helpless woman by violating an order so lovingly established.

It would have been useless to have attempted to explain such thoughts to Philip, and fortunately she did not have to. He had made up his mind to leave Gayton for quite different reasons. He had a wife, he had a daughter, he would soon, he hoped, have a son. It was time finally to settle down, to do what was in his blood and farm his own land. He started to look round for suitable properties close to his old haunts in north Norfolk, to receive lengthy particulars in fat folders and to attend auctions in Norwich.

Maria found out that it was the housemaid, Fanny Bell, who had spelt 'Welcome the Bride' on the pincushion. Her heart warmed to her from that moment, and now Fanny showed such fondness for Helena and skill in handling her that she was promoted to become her nurse. Philip had assumed that his wife's announcement that she intended to write had been a passing whim. At first he was dismayed to hear that she spent so much time scribbling, but when she told him that what she was writing was not a novel but fairy stories, and that even if they were published she would see to it that they did not come out under her own name, he was entirely satisfied.

Madame was shocked to discover from her researches that the name 'Gayton' was probably derived from a word meaning 'a wet place' and horrified to learn that water could actually be seen not a hundred yards from one of the upper windows. Therefore, while she thought farming one of the most expensive hobbies in the world for a gentleman and Philip an absolute fool to waste his money on it, she thoroughly endorsed their plans to move.

Maria had not wanted her first baby to be born at Bridge House. For her second she made arrangements long in advance, persuading Philip how much better it would be for her health if they all went to Bournemouth for the winter; how easily Mrs. Compton could find them a furnished house, how sensible to be near Madame before they made their final move.

In fact Philip was already negotiating to buy an estate which he had known all his life and longed to possess. By chance up for sale at this exact moment, it lay off the road between Erpingham and the little market town of Aylsham, and he had passed its gates since he was a boy. It was a modest property of about four hundred acres of excellent farmland with coverts for shooting. In the Middle Ages it had been an outlying manor belonging to the monks of Bury St. Edmunds, given to the abbey by King John on the condition it provided four wax candles to burn night and day round the shrine of St. Edmund.

Once it had been surrounded by clusters of conical hives, the bees foraging across the river in the quiet fields later to lie beneath the Jacobean splendour of Blickling Hall. But when the great abbey fell the medieval manor house was abandoned and partially ruined. The new owners, caring as little for shrines as they did for damp, built another Abbots Hall on rising ground the opposite side of the road. This was the small square, red brick house that Philip had always coveted and to which he now added another wing.

Although the place had been modernized, it remained surrounded by a medley of seventeenth-century buildings, untidy survivors from a self-sufficient economy. There was a blacksmith's forge where horseshoes still hung on the walls, a brew house with a brick oven, a carpenter's shop, marble-shelved larders, dairies, a long row of stables with lofts above and a fine thatched barn overlooking the pond. There was an orchard, too, and a walled garden and a tree-lined drive with a wood at the end of it where in spring the lilies of the valley grew. Here the rooks had made their home and their continuous caw provided a melancholy counterpoint to the daily life of the family.

Just in sight of the house were the farm workers' cottages. In front of these was common land and with hitched skirts the women carried their buckets down to the river past donkeys, ducks and geese. The river was the Bure, and it wound its way through the grounds, over water meadows and by pasture, sheltering perch and tench and fat brown trout feeding among the weeds.

The front windows looked across a lawn and herbaceous borders to the distant spire of Aylsham church. To the north, the grey flint tower of Banningham rose from the middle of the cornfields. Even now Abbots Hall is remote. Then it stood away from the world in a land of pastel shades, gentle undulations and large skies. Anything more different from the peaks of the Apennines or the brilliance of the Côte d'Azur could hardly be imagined. Yet in many ways it was a sunny house and in hot summers the fruit of the passion flower ripened on the

south wall. For other people, other temperaments, circumstances and desires, it could have been a paradise.

For Philip Shepheard, signing the contract at his solicitor's
in Aylsham market place, paradise was a strictly theological
concept. But he was exceedingly happy. In Bournemouth
Pasqua had given birth to a son, called after himself. Soon he
would be living in a house he had always longed to have,
farming his own land, shooting his own coverts, fishing his
own river, seeing to the wise management of an estate which in
the fullness of time he would hand on intact to his children.

In October 1884, they moved in. Maria Pasqua was delighted
to leave Bridge House. Mrs. Woods had been given notice, the
only Gayton servant she brought with her was Nana, her
former housemaid, Fanny Bell. At last Ellen's dead hand had
been lifted. That a good deal of her furniture should come with
them was inescapable, but now Maria could arrange it as she
pleased. Her fairy tales had been accepted by a publisher, she
was the mother of a son, she was twenty-eight years old and full
of energy. After careful thought Philip came to the conclusion
that the house was too small for his growing family, so he
decided to add another wing, the top floor to be the nursery,
the bottom his wife's drawing-room. Helena was three-and-a-
half. She just remembered their arrival because the workmen
were still in the house and she had to sleep on a mattress on the
floor.

Philip had a new staircase made, panelled in oak the dining-
room and hall, and bought a massive dining-room table and
sideboard. The furnishing of the new drawing-room was left
entirely to Maria. She filled it with a mixture of Simson and
Shepheard things, Persian carpets, looking glasses, branched
candlesticks, fluted corner cupboards painted in blue and gold,
buttoned velvet sofas and circular tables. The only photograph
in the room was one of Madame. A guardian presence surrounded by purple plush, she sat bolt upright in her chair

flanked by lilies. She held a fan in her hand and at her feet crouched a black labrador.

Outside, close to the new wing, Maria Pasqua had a large greenhouse built. Here she was always warm, generally alone, queen of the flowers, absolute mistress of her plants. She grew plumbagoes, trained bougainvillaeas on wires, and hung baskets of bright geraniums from the roof. She was happy in the moist hot air, smelling and feeling her flowers, watering them, moving their positions on the slatted shelves, explaining gently to inquirers that not all living things get on with their neighbours.

Her book had been published in a series which declared itself suitable for birthday presents, school prizes and family rewards. She called herself 'Pan' which pleased Philip as it was the name of one of his favourite dogs. She subscribed to a press cutting agency but the reviews were few. The tales disappeared almost without trace except for a small number of complimentary copies, still bright in their fawn covers, discovered in a bedroom drawer nearly a hundred years later.

Maria Pasqua had been at Abbots Hall for three months only when she conceived again. All her energies were now directed towards her children, to Helena and Phil and the new baby. He was born in November and called Samuel after Philip's eldest brother, the former vicar of Calthorpe. She was determined to make the day nursery as bright and cheerful as she could so that the children would be surrounded from their earliest years by colour and their imaginations stimulated by what they saw. For a long time she had been collecting pictures from catalogues, cards, magazines and the Christmas numbers of the *Illustrated London News*. These she cut out and placed in a trunk. There they remained, the soldier in red and gold, the horses and the coachmen, the kittens, the little girl in blue and the birds of paradise until the day came when they were taken out to be pasted on the wall.

Maria and Nana placed a circle of chairs in the middle of the nursery, gave the children toys and told them that they must remain inside. Phil. was too young to understand, but safe behind the barricade Helena watched her mother's eager face as she trimmed the pictures, the little slithers of paper falling on to the carpet like nailparings while Nana stirred the thick paste. To her joy, Maria found she had enough pictures left over to cover the walls of the night nursery as well. Her children would wake up in the morning to a world of life and amusement.

The varnish was barely dry before the household was thrown into a state of alarm and confusion. A special messenger arrived from Yarmouth to say that Madame de Noailles had come there in a friend's yacht and wished to see Mrs. Shepheard.

Maria was tired, she was still nursing Samuel, she felt depressed and quite unable to face the journey or endure the pressure of Madame's company. But if she did not go Madame might come to Abbots Hall, and she was as terrified of that as Philip was determined to prevent it. The year before Madame had threatened to do so and had asked that before her arrival all the trees near the house should be cut down and cows brought up from the farm and tethered at the open windows during the day so that everyone could benefit from their wholesome breath. Apart from these directions, they both knew that once she actually saw Abbots Hall and grasped the proximity of the river and pond they would be ordered to sell up immediately and move to a healthier spot. Fortunately the wind shifted, the yacht had to put to sea and Madame staved off bronchitis only by eating plate after plate of soft herring roes.

The voyage over, she wrote from Holywell Lodge to express her disappointment and to demand their presence at Eastbourne. To prevent Maria suffering from eyestrain she had ordered green curtains to be put up in every room she was likely to enter. She was also having a hole cut in Maria's bedroom door so that she could see the children asleep without opening it. Miss Roche was sent to dispatch a telegram, laboriously transcribed by a disconcerted clerk at Aylsham post office and received by Philip with some irritation: 'Madame sends saloon carriage with cot in which she came from Cornwall without fatigue. Hopes Maria will try it. Saloon will arrive Aylsham Tuesday. Bring you here same day. All charges are paid. Answer paid. Roche.'

Saloon carriages were a rarity at Aylsham. There was quite a crowd to see them off. The under-nurse came as well because even the sight of a train made Nana ill, and indeed she ruined the dignity of the occasion by being sick out of the window before they had even left the station.

Their carriage went straight through to its destination without changing. Maria spent all the time in the hammock swaying gently to the rhythm of the wheels and dreaming that she was back at Cannes among swallows and the oleanders, the red carnations and the apricots, the clatter of empty buckets and the voices of sailors greeting each other across a dancing sea. She could hardly believe it when they told her that they had arrived at Eastbourne.

ELEVEN

Such were the preliminaries to many visits to Holywell Lodge. Madame was in a constant state of agitation over Maria's health and particularly anxious about the adverse effects of the cold Norfolk spring upon her delicate throat. She consulted Dr. Wilkinson, who sent down a new invention for her use. This consisted of a stand which contained about eight bottles holding liquids of various colours. According to a timetable and the condition of her chest, Maria had to inhale from the bottles through a long rubber tube. In the afternoon, with hands washed, hair combed and wearing a clean white pinafore and bows, Helena was allowed downstairs to sit beside her. When her mother had finished breathing in the vapour, Helena would gently brush her hair.

She loved her mother devotedly and would wait by the nursery door to catch the sound of her footsteps so that she would be the first to fling herself into her arms. Maria Pasqua would sit in the rocking chair and tell them stories. They spoke to each other in French. Although, on the surface, her household differed little from others of the same kind, perhaps an unconscious repudiation of the country of her adoption determined Maria that her children should be bilingual. To this end she first employed a French under-nurse who knew no English, and later a French governess. Her children thought in French, dreamed in French, and to the end of their lives would speak it automatically in times of stress.

Apart from tales of her life in the mountains, her experiences in Rome with Domenico and the long trek to Paris, the story the children most often wanted to hear happened when their mother was a child and Madame had a house in the Pyrenees. One of her Standish relations was staying in the house and on a cold winter's night he had to visit the gentleman's lavatory which was outside. This was familiar to Helena, Phil and Samuel, since on the grounds of economy, their father had refused to instal more than one flushing lavatory at Abbots Hall and during the day he and any male guests would disappear into the garden to visit an earth closet. Madame's Standish relation, however, found himself in a situation unlikely to occur at Aylsham. About to open the door he heard to his utter horror what he thought to be the sniffing of a wolf. A minute later his fears were confirmed as a ghastly howl rent the night. For hour after hour the wolf prowled round and round intent upon his prey. Too far from the house for his cries to be heard, the unfortunate man was discovered in the morning, half dead with cold.

To Helena's relief, however, he was nursed back to health and this marked the difference between Maria Pasqua's stories and those of her father. Philip loved his children, but he had little imagination and no sympathy whatsoever with the fears of the young. No Norfolk child cares to go out alone at night for dread of meeting Black Shuck, the great dark dog from Scandinavia with burning eyes and bloody mouth who relentlessly treads the coast road from Lynn to Yarmouth before circling inland to pad his way through sleeping villages.

Philip took a grim pleasure in playing upon these fears. He tried constantly and vainly to persuade and even to bribe his children to walk alone to the end of the drive after sunset. There was something in his make-up which relished the macabre and obtained satisfaction from contemplating the consequences of either crime or folly. When he first came to Abbots Hall he found a rusty barred door which had been taken from

Norwich jail. He placed this by the orchard wall, where it cast its sinister shadow across the carefree path to the swing.

His taste contributed to the rather sombre atmosphere of the house. He had inherited a lantern salvaged from the man o'war *Peggy*, lost off the Haseboro's with all hands the previous century. Maria Pasqua wanted to keep it in the garden as a home for her doves. Philip insisted upon hanging it from a beam in the hall close to the lamp which the notorious murderer, James Rush, had carried with him on the night of the crime.

Sitting in his armchair by the side of the fire in the dining-room, the children in a row on a backless bench before the flames, he would tell them the story of Jack and the Beanstalk and sometimes sing them snatches of old ballads he had learnt long ago in the schoolmaster's house at Roughton. He enjoyed reading aloud 'The Ancient Mariner' or 'The Dream of Eugene Aram', but most of all he delighted to tell a tale about a boy who had once lived at Erpingham. It was a true story. There was no escape, no happy ending and it did not concern a remote region like the Pyrenees but a village the children knew well as the home of their father's boyhood and the resting place of so many of their forebears.

In that churchyard there was a large table tomb that had been allowed to fall into a bad state of repair and develop gaping cracks on the stone slab which covered it. Once, in the reign of George III, when their father's mother was a girl, one of the village boys told another that he would give him a shilling if he dared to go into the churchyard at night and stick his pocket knife into one of those cracks.

The boy took on the bet and when the hour came was seen off from his cottage door by his companion. Clutching in his hand a large knife with an open blade the boy made his way slowly down the deserted street. The church with its great tower lies apart from the village, majestic and lonely in its fields.

Reluctantly the boy left the safety of the road and walked up the narrow lane in the darkness past the tossing arms of the elm trees, through the lychgate and into the churchyard. He knew exactly where the tomb was, approached it as fast as he could, raised his knife and struck it down hard into one of the cracks. But in his haste and fear he had not noticed that when he raised his arm his coat brushed the top of the tomb. The knife caught its edge and when the boy turned for home he felt a tugging behind him, a hand coming out of the grave and holding him fast. In the morning he was found dead, the knife still through his coat. He had died of fright.

These stories were told in the long evenings after Christmas and Helena held Phil's hand and was glad of the warmth of his body. Maria Pasqua hated the cold northern winters. She would tell her children over and over again that she was an exile in a strange country, an Israelite wandering in the wilderness. One day she would return to Italy and of course they would all come too. Then they would live among her own people in that promised land of singing and dancing where the sun always shone and grapes could be picked by the wayside.

Especially she loathed November and December and the first eight weeks of the year. These were Philip's favourite months. He thoroughly enjoyed the winter and looked forward to it. He loved waiting for duck by the river, walking in the woods and fields and visiting the cattle in their shed at the farm. When he went out shooting he used often to put the game on the lawn opposite the nursery windows so that the children could see it. Sometimes he would come upstairs and show it to them, drawing attention to the plumage of a cock pheasant and the powerful breast muscles of a duck.

Maria Pasqua hated to see the limp feathers and the milky dead eyes. She pitied the impotent claws and the dry tracery of the webbed feet. Once in the late afternoon of an autumn day a man came to the house leading a bear. Philip was delighted. He called the children down and told them to wrap up and watch from the porch. The bear was enormous and attached to his master by a chain. He was muzzled and balanced a pole in his elbow. His coat was dull and smelt of sour straw and above the cone of the muzzle the eyes were sly and wary. Maria Pasqua disliked performing animals or to see any creature in captivity. She spoke in French to Philip who, disappointed, paid the man to go away.

With one part of her Maria wished above all things to be a good wife and mother, to accommodate herself to her husband and live like any other English woman in her position. But with the other she was rebellious, frustrated and bored. She shared none of Philip's interests and he none of hers. She was amusing and lively, so quick that she understood people's feelings before they did themselves, whereas he was slow, quiet, extremely reserved and never noticed the reactions of others. She hated or loved in an instant. He was cautious in his judgements, inflexible, and upright. She was impulsive and generous, he careful to the point of meanness. She expanded like a flower in the company of others, he preferred to be alone. She loved poetry and novels, he read the *Lancet* and the *Horse and Hound*.

The days of Ascot, Henley or the Derby were over. Jaunts to Switzerland, tours of Wales, visits to the London theatre and consultations with his tailor in Hanover Street belonged to another existence. He sat on the Bench, went once a week to Norwich market, occasionally to shooting parties. Except for reluctant visits to Madame he rarely left home and entertained his neighbours very infrequently.

After Samuel's birth Maria was at her loveliest. Madame had seen to it that she had money of her own and she ordered her best dresses and hats from Paris. In those early years Philip occasionally accepted one of the numerous invitations to a local garden party. One summer she walked over the lawn to say goodbye to the children before going. She had on a black hat with most delicately coloured yellow roses and a black silk dress. Watching her crossing the grass, a graceful, eager figure with the brim of her hat shading her face, Helena ran to her, thinking she was the most beautiful person she had ever seen.

It was not only her children who thought so. Gifted with charm as well as beauty, Maria Pasqua was the natural centre of attention in any gathering. Awareness of the sadness of life gave edge to her laughter. Philip admired her vivacity and his eyes shone as he watched her, but she knew, and knew with resentment, that he wanted her to be attractive to him alone. As responsive to admiration as a sea anemone to the tugging of the tide, she allowed herself to flirt just a little with the middle-aged contemporaries of her husband. Philip never let her out of his sight. When he saw her surrounded by a group of men he would come up at once to join the conversation and so put an effective stop to it. If other people looked at his wife, she had better stay at home.

As time went on he became more and more absorbed in his own pursuits and reluctant to do any entertaining whatsoever. All he wanted in the evening was his armchair, his *Times*, and his slippers. He smoked a pipe and had a tumbler at his side with a very little whisky in it. By the light of a single oil lamp Maria sat reading or sewing. There was no conversation.

Maria knew that she was losing touch both with her friends at Bournemouth and the coterie which surrounded Madame de Noailles. How could she explain life at Aylsham to Pauline von Hügel, or expect even kind Mrs. Compton to understand that her husband allowed her only a single oil lamp in the evening and that they went to bed at nine?

It was not that she altogether disliked her surroundings or was unoccupied. She loved the beauties of nature and enjoyed wandering by the river or through the water meadows where the wild daffodils grew in March. She taught her children to know and appreciate the flowers and birds, and would take them past their private gate by the rookery to look for the nests of the mallards and to pick the yellow marigolds. There was no need for Madame to urge her to visit her husband's tenants. The fact that the women curtsied to her did not mean that she had forgotten that she had been born much poorer than they. If anyone at the cottages was ill, she was the first to call. She knew all the children by name, remembered birthdays and Christmas hampers, and would listen to their problems with spontaneous sympathy.

What she wanted from Madame was not advice but exchange of ideas, gossip about people and the latest publications. Unfortunately however, she had married a man who farmed and Madame was given a splendid opportunity to air her own obsessions. Her letters concentrated not upon books but the production of pure food and the waste of wind power. Philip must invite a party of farmers and millers to Abbots Hall. They should be given a cold luncheon and a chance to compare Maria's homemade bread with the unwholesome stuff they produced from foreign flour. Why did not Maria accompany Philip to an agricultural meeting and say a few words in her beautiful English on clean cow sheds and the absolute necessity to rebuild our decaying windmills?

Maria cared nothing for flour or windmills. Longing for a more demonstrative husband, for companionship, for larger horizons, for life itself, she started to write a novel. She wrote for hours every day, pouring out her frustrations, hopes, desires and observations of human nature into a large notebook. Coming downstairs in her clean pinafore, Helena was told that she must sit absolutely quiet. The notebook was three-quarters filled and Helena watched her mother's absorbed face and her eager pen followed by pauses for thought. Suddenly there was no more writing. The notebook disappeared and Helena asked what had happened. She had burnt it all, her mother answered, she could not bear to think of anyone else reading it. Helena was overcome both by disappointment at the waste of so much effort and grief for the evident emotions that had promoted it. She was only seven. She sensed what she could not articulate and asked no questions.

The truth of the matter was that Maria Pasqua understood the feelings of everyone in the world except those of her husband. For his part, half wilfully, half stupidly, he was blind to her needs and paid the price for it.

TWELVE

Philip's dislike of entertaining became so pronounced that before long almost the only visitors he tolerated at Abbots Hall were members of his own family. Since he was the youngest son and had married a girl eighteen years his junior, the children of his brothers and sisters were the same age as his wife. His own children, therefore, had no first cousins of their own age at all and even if they had, Philip probably would have grudged the expense of amusing them.

Provided that he was not expected to exert himself, he remained however on amiable terms with his relations and from a distance followed their careers with much interest. He was glad that his godson, Philip Paston Mack, was settling down so well in the 12th Lancers and that his cousin Alfred Cooper was making such a successful career for himself as a London surgeon. But that was as far as it went. His own social or professional ambitions had dissolved long ago, his world contracted to the tangible enjoyments and petty responsibilities of a small landowner. It was, in his opinion, dishonourable to accept invitations one had no intention of reciprocating. So pretty Nellie Mack beckoned in vain from Paston, the music sounded over lawns untrodden by Maria Pasqua and the candles of the evening parties never lit up her face.

The only relations the children saw regularly were their father's spinster sisters Charlotte and Betty and his eldest brother Sam, who all lived together at Erpingham House. Conversion to the Catholic Church had not altered Parson

Sam. Like his brother Philip and his sisters, once having given his allegiance to Rome, he practised his faith meticulously, but it was rarely spoken of and never paraded. In the past he had not dressed much like a clergyman nor allowed Holy Orders to interfere with his pleasures. Too old now to hunt, he still appreciated his bottle and the company of an attractive woman.

He had been born in the first year of the reign of George IV and his manners and way of speaking belonged to another age. On Christmas Day he would arrive at Abbots Hall in his dog cart while Charlotte and Betty followed in a very old-fashioned low carriage. It was the only day in the year that Philip allowed a fire to be lit in the hall and ordered his best port up from the cellar. He and his brother sat sideways at the end of the dinner table cracking walnuts and sipping port and then Sam would rise to his feet and drink Maria's health in a ceremonious speech.

Early on Christmas morning Philip took the pulse of each child and put the information down at the back of his diary. He then took them singly through the passage which led to the kitchens and measured their height carefully against the wall, ruling an exact line and marking the name, age and date. They were allowed downstairs again for the dessert and listened to their uncle's speech with admiration. In his time he had been a good classical scholar and Helena noticed once that his eyes filled with tears when Phil and Samuel recited some Latin verses they had learnt at school and which reminded him of his youth at Cambridge.

He hated anything that he thought savoured of pretentiousness and when she was a little older used to torment Helena by threatening to visit her at her fashionable convent wearing his old clothes and carrying the digger which he never left behind him in the country. Although, unlike his sisters, he admired Maria Pasqua, he would tease her by driving up to the front door in the farm gig with pigs under the net, saying he liked the smell of manure which he knew she detested.

Charlotte and Betty were less often at Aylsham. Time had done nothing to soften the impression they had formed of Maria on the afternoon when she had come to Bridge House as a bride. Philip never spoke of Ellen. Nor did they, but Maria felt they had not forgotten her and sometimes, sitting talking stiffly in her drawing-room she would see their eyes slide from the rich plush of Madame's photograph to the rosewood work table where Ellen had once kept her sewing.

They considered the notion of French nurses and governesses affected and disliked to hear their niece and nephews chatter to one another in a foreign tongue. Clothed themselves not merely simply but in such an old-fashioned manner as to make the urchins in North Walsham snigger, they thought it absurdly extravagant of their sister-in-law not to employ a local dress-maker. No doubt in the old days people had stood on chairs to look at Pasqua, but Aylsham was not Paris and chairs had been made for a more useful purpose.

Yet they were good people. If they could have understood Maria Pasqua, they would have done. Once a year they invited Philip and his wife and children to Erpingham for the day. Helena looked forward to it. She would have been completely happy in the company of her father's relations if it had not been for the awareness of her mother's tedium.

They drove the two miles between Abbots Hall and Erpingham House in the wagonette. Occasionally they took the longer way past some ponds where Philip said a woman who had committed suicide when he was a boy could still be heard shrieking in the mist of November evenings. Usually they went past the lane which led to the church, and Helena would get out to open the large white gate to allow the wagonette to go up the long drive over grassland dotted with trees which included the Duke of Wellington's oak.

Erpingham House was built in the reign of Queen Anne and was much more beautiful than Abbots Hall. The drive ended in a circular sweep before a cedar, and as soon as they heard the carriage Parson Sam together with Charlotte and Betty and the spaniel came out to greet them while the old coachman took the horse's head.

The hall smelt of musk, which hung in a cascade over the rails at the top of the staircase. They took off their coats and hats in Charlotte's bedroom and Helena looked round at once for the cuckoo clock. When she was very small she thought the bird might be alive and waited anxiously for it to come out and to bow low before speaking. She could not understand how or upon what it lived and she would not have gone into the bedroom at all if her mother had not been with her.

Betty's room was next door. On the table near her bed she had placed a real skull with some crossbones fixed on the wall under a large crucifix. Maria told Helena that Susanna had a brooch like it and that her Aunt Betty had placed the skull there to remind her of death. She disliked it heartily herself and would not dream of having it anywhere near her at Aylsham. Helena felt as her mother did but secretly admired her aunt's bravery.

Parson Sam's room faced the front of the house. Hanging on his wall was a notice in large lettering which read, 'The Folly and Imbecility of Mankind are Infinite'. Helena thought it was a text from the Bible. Life was to teach her that this early assumption was substantially correct.

An impatient prodding with his digger on the gravel outside meant that Uncle Sam was ready to take Helena to see the barn and the old sow. In the yard he found a little trolley which was used for carrying sacks and he wheeled her up and down the barn floor in it while she yelled with delight. Leaving Maria Pasqua to talk with Betty, Charlotte came out to show Helena her own garden with its canary creeper, then took her to the back door to get food for the hens, to talk to the cook and watch the dairy maid remove the wrinkled cream from the flat milk pans.

The most important event of the day was the meal. Before the gong sounded Charlotte and Betty retired upstairs to put on lace caps adorned with large black bows while Rebecca, the parlour maid, saw to it that Helena was placed at table opposite the cupboard that contained the blue lustre jugs.

Afterwards Parson Sam took Philip round the farm and Maria Pasqua sat in the drawing-room where once old Mack had come to woo Susanna. She watched Helena's rapt face as, perched on a stool, she pored over her Aunt Charlotte's album. Charlotte herself, pleased at the interest taken, had put on a small pair of wire spectacles. She leant over Helena, reading aloud and turning over the pages:

> 'Sweet Shepherdess, to receive such a prize,
> At once thrilled each nerve with delight.
> It occasioned in me the sweetest surprise
> My pleasure no words could recite.'

'That's you,' Helena said. 'You're the shepherdess.' Charlotte looked delighted. She remarked that in those days gentlemen wrote such things in young ladies' albums as a matter of course. But yes, he was quite a poet.

Maria Pasqua wondered what prize Charlotte had given him. She looked at her large nose and was momentarily taken aback to think that she had ever had an admirer. She was grateful for her sisters-in-law's kindness, for the trouble they had taken to give Helena her favourite boiled custard and to place her opposite the lustre jugs. She knew that they had about them a kind of firmness and serenity which she could never match. She was ashamed of her own feelings, at the mixture of envy and irritation she felt at the thought of life going on so peacefully in that house long before she was born. She almost resented the rhythm of their days; nothing but ducks and hens, chickens and eggs, seed time and harvest, the cows and calving and the quiet acceptance that Philip's mother should have twelve children and die at the end of it all because a bungling village midwife had dirty hands. Who could she talk about such things with? Philip never. Not with her children until it was too late and she had nothing to say.

Betty's voice cut through Charlotte's. Her brother William's wife, Jenny, was so careless. Pasqua would never believe it but frequently she forgot to lock up the house, even at night. With all that silver! And the servants were often elsewhere during the day. Anyone could creep into the hall and steal it. 'That's what we used to call a charade,' Charlotte was saying to Helena. 'A riddle really. It was put in by our brother Martin, the one who was lost at sea.'

The expression on Helena's face, an oval foreign face like her mother's, hovered between excitement and pity. Drowned? Yes. He had joined the Navy and when he was a young man had been swept overboard one night in an Atlantic gale. In an instant Maria Pasqua translated the spidery brown writing into flesh. A good-looking boy with that rich curling Shepheard hair, little fingers with short grubby nails painfully copying his riddle on to the page his elder sister had ruled for him.

'So,' Betty went on, 'Charlotte and I decided to teach Jenny a lesson. One morning, when we knew she was out, we went and took some of the best pieces back here and locked them in a cupboard. It wasn't until the next day that Jenny missed them and rushed over to tell us of the theft. Naturally,' Betty added, looking severely at Maria, 'we kept her in suspense and gave her a good talking to before we told her where her silver actually was.'

'Naturally,' Maria said, noticing the changed light between the layered branches of the cedar and straining her ears for the return of her husband and the footsteps of Rebecca bearing the Georgian teapot.

THIRTEEN

As the children grew up they became increasingly aware of the contrast between the atmosphere of sophisticated eccentricity which surrounded Madame de Noailles and the uneventful routine of their Norfolk existence. Not for a moment did Madame release her hold upon them, not for a day relax her efforts to improve Maria's health, purify Philip's cowsheds and regulate the children's education.

She was rewriting her will and intended to leave Maria a substantial annuity provided that she promised always to wear white in the summer and never to put on laced shoes. She was sending them three dozen bottles of Bordeaux and fifty bottles of port. Maria must drink the port with a little sugar in it exactly at sundown. But in order for it to be efficacious, soft rainwater recovered from the roof by the servants should be added. Philip must supervise its collection.

The arrangements for the journey to Holywell Lodge were now put into the hands of her cousin, Arthur Jephson. Captain Jephson had recently returned from Africa where, at Madame's prompting, he had commanded a detachment of Stanley's expedition for the relief of Emin Pasha. It was he who now had to organize the special coach and see to it that Maria's hammock was comfortably slung.

In her own peculiar way and on her own terms, Madame was very kind. But the children remained not merely in awe of her but oppressively conscious of their mother's constraint. If their aunts thought of Maria Pasqua as a parakeet which had

99

in the garden Phil was expected to climb the tree and actually had his cup handed to him by Madame herself.

Phil was not the only one to be frightened by Madame. All the children did their best to avoid meeting her either in the house or grounds. Should they do so, they followed their mother's instructions and came forward quietly to kiss her hand. If they were lucky she merely bowed, smiled and went on her regal way. If they were not, she would inquire about their reading, their arithmetic, the difference between an isthmus and a peninsula, or ask them to perform some small service. Sometimes she gave them scissors and told them to cut off the dead roses. This task terrified Helena. Wearing a long trailing dress, hook nose protruding from beneath a silk shawl which she wore over her head, Madame would walk a few paces behind, watching to see that the right roses were cut.

She then usually retired to a tent which she had had erected for herself on one side of the law with its open flaps facing south. The children were warned that on no account must they go near the tent when Madame was in it. The fact was that Madame de Noailles was an early sunbather. Once inside the tent she would remove most of her clothes to allow the beneficial rays to play over her body.

When they saw her go into her tent the children knew they were safe for a while. Sometimes they would creep upstairs into her bedroom to look out of the red windows their father had told them about. Fascinated, they would stand for as long as they dared staring out on to a world where everything was literally *couleur de rose*, where the lawn looked like a burning desert and the trees as if on fire.

At other times they would go stealthily into the drawing-room to inspect the large square picture by Sir Thomas Lawrence of Madame's American grandmother, the first Mrs. Henry Baring, and her children. They knew nothing of its value or artistic merit: what attracted them was something which was not there.

Mrs. Baring, negligently dressed with her hair over her shoulders, sat near her little daughter at one end of a sofa. At the other end her son knelt with his arms round the neck of an exceedingly fierce-looking dog. Between the boy and his mother there was a dark space. In that space, so Miss Roche whispered to the children, had sat Henry Baring himself. After the divorce, Miss Roche would continue with pursed lips, Mrs. Baring requested Lawrence to paint out the offending figure of her husband. The three children would examine the picture carefully, puzzled at the idea of a divorce, wondering where, when he was there, Henry Baring had put his legs, and what kind of dog it was to have a muzzle which looked like something between a bear and a lion.

Holywell Lodge was separated from the Downs by a narrow road only; Madame owned part of the Downs and her sheep grazed there. As a result of this the household lived almost entirely on mutton, of which the children grew very tired. The mutton was kept in a meat safe attached to a tree at the back of the house. It was of Madame's design and raised to a considerable height by means of a rope and pulley. This contraption had a particular interest for the children not merely because of its mechanics and the familiar burden it held, but because it had a story connected with it which their mother had often told them.

Once, when Maria Pasqua was young and had first come to England, Madame had had a manservant called Frederick whose special task it was to raise and lower the pulley. She was very proud of the hygienic manner in which she kept her meat and was fond of showing her invention to visitors.

On one occasion a French general was being entertained, and as usual Madame took him off to see where his dinner was kept. Frederick was commanded to pull the rope but instead of doing so, he threw himself upon his knees before the general crying 'Pardon, mon general, pardon!' No one could make out what on earth had happened. At last, bursting into sobs, Frederick explained that he was a deserter from the French army and had thought Madame had summoned the general to have him shot.

If a constant diet of mutton made their meals boring, Madame's insistence that the children should eat with her in the dining-room turned luncheon into an ordeal. Madame sat at a special table by herself and had a small screen about two feet high placed round her plate so that no one could watch her eating. She told the children that she had the screen put there so that they could not see her picking the bones. Maria Pasqua said the real reason was that she was enjoying special dishes. Occasionally she would poke her face out from behind the screen to make some remark or ask the children some question which they were too frightened to answer.

On the whole, despite Madame's genuine affection and Miss Roche's attempts to amuse them, the children were extremely relieved when their visit came to an end and they were allowed to go home and see their father. Philip sulked if he had to accompany them; if he remained where he was he complained of desertion. Yet it was to him that Madame turned when Miss Roche fell seriously ill. The letter arrived when they were all at Aylsham and Philip left for Eastbourne at once. He had always respected Miss Roche, partly because she had been good to Pasqua and partly because he pitied her dependence upon Madame de Noailles.

Miss Roche died shortly after his arrival at Holywell Lodge. Through the servants and nurses morbid gossip about her last moments filtered back to the children. She had fought for her life like a tiger, she had had visions of the devil and suffocated at the last, choked to death by her own screams. Madame, moreover, hated corpses so much that hardly had the breath left the body before it was bundled into a coffin and placed upside down in the coach house.

Three weeks later Madame wrote to Maria to say she missed Miss Roche very much and begged them all to come and stay. Helena was terrified of going. Death now seemed as horrible to her as they said it had been to Madame. It was grey and repellent, smelling like a sodden wasps' nest dug up by the gardener's spade. It had nothing to do with God or angels or heaven's gate, only with choking, screaming, and poor Miss Roche's thin body upside down in a coach house.

She dreaded the return to Holywell Lodge and the first sight of a house where anyone had died, let alone Miss Roche who only a little while ago had helped her to embroider a sunflower on to a piece of cardboard. She sat with Phil and Samuel in the cab driving across Eastbourne and held her mother's hand tightly, comforted only by the sight of the large bottles of blue and green coloured water in a chemist's window. Maria Pasqua noticed the colours too, and remembered a journey to Cannes, a translucent sea, the foyer of an hotel, and the kiss of a woman left behind to exercise the dogs.

It was not until she was very much older that Helena learnt the truth about Miss Roche's tragic end.

After her death, a will signed by Madame leaving her thousands of pounds was discovered under her pillow. Although by far the elder of the two, she had convinced herself that she would survive Madame and live to enjoy both independence and plenty. Knowing how frequently Madame changed her will, only too conscious of the vagaries and impulsive inconsistencies of her temperament, she determined that come what may, she would keep in her employer's good graces. Far beyond the usual age for retirement, she wore herself out trying to please, and when she knew she was ill refused either to see a doctor or to go to bed.

She kept on her feet as long as she was able, and when at last she collapsed it was too late. All Philip could do was to urge Madame to call the priest so that she could receive the Last Sacraments. This Madame willingly agreed to, but when the priest entered the bedroom Miss Roche's clouded mind gave way to fear. She called out over and over again that she could not go to Confession because she knew for certain that Madame was listening at the door. Philip assured her that this was not the case and that he would stand in the stairway to see that she was left absolutely alone. It was to no avail. The priest had to go, and terrified of Madame to the end, Miss Roche slipped into unconsciousness and death.

At Madame's request, Philip went through her papers. She seemed to have no relations and it turned out that there was some mystery about her birth and upbringing. He would never reveal to Pasqua what it was.

FOURTEEN

After Miss Roche's death Madame decided to live permanently in the South of France. She bought two houses, one for the winter at Costebelle, near Hyères, the other for the hot weather not far away at Carqueiranne. In case she wanted to visit England she kept on Holywell Lodge with a married couple called Albert and Elizabeth in charge. She liked the idea of extending hospitality even in her absence and wished to be able to provide a seaside holiday to those whose lives or aspirations merited it.

In many ways Maria was glad that Madame had left England. It was unlikely now that she would swoop down upon them at Abbots Hall, and the little errands and small services she expected from Philip were of necessity diminished. Maria hoped that they would now be able to enjoy long holidays at Eastbourne free from the constraint of Madame's presence. But she reckoned without her husband's obstinacy. She found it almost impossible to persuade him to leave Norfolk.

Madame begged them to stay at Holywell Lodge for months at a time. She especially urged them to go there in the autumn as the country was so unhealthy at the fall of leaf and the fall of *oak leaves* was particularly unwholesome. Albert and Elizabeth had been told to wait upon them hand and foot and Philip could shoot partridge on the Downs. It would be doing her a kindness, she urgently wanted Philip's advice about her cows, one of which Albert had already allowed to die of constipation.

Philip refused. Pasqua could go, of course, and the children.

There was nothing to prevent them, although why they wanted to leave their own home to live in someone else's house was beyond his understanding. At last he was getting his property running as he wished. He had patched up the medieval farm-house, repaired the thatched roof of the barn, rebuilt the cow-sheds and, most important of all, converted a small building in the grounds into a chapel.

Because she was born to it and her temperament was different, Maria's religion was not so precise or practised so punctili-ously as Philip's. To her, Catholicism was as natural as breath-ing, to him something which had been acquired. She was content to read a passage from the New Testament every evening by lamplight, scribbling comments in the margin. She instructed the children and heard Mass whenever she could, but he fretted because he could not go to Confession and Com-munion every week.

In those days Catholics in Norfolk were few and unpopular. It was difficult to find a place to hear Mass; the nearest priest lived miles away at Cromer, where as yet there was no church, and Mass had to be celebrated in a room at the Red Lion Hotel. It took the family a long time to get there from Aylsham and sometimes in the winter, when they reached the slope leading into the town, Philip would insist that everyone should get out and walk the rest of the way for fear of straining the horses.

Now they had a chapel of their own. Maria embroidered the altar cloths, made hosts out of unleavened bread, and the Bishop arrived to say the first Mass to be celebrated at Aylsham since the Reformation. After that the little chapel was served from time to time by Jesuits from Yarmouth whom Philip allowed to stay in the house. Such, however, was the hostility to Catholics which still lingered in the neighbourhood, that he was advised to delay erecting the cross he had intended to set above the door.

The family from Erpingham attended the chapel as often as

they could. One July, when Helena was nine, she heard her Uncle Sam's dogcart on the gravel and rushed out to meet him. He would never be more surprised in his life, she said, but God had suddenly decided to give them all a new baby brother. Sam blessed his soul, jingled the coins in his pocket, looked anxious and went in to find Philip.

Maria Pasqua had not wanted another child. The birth was long and difficult and she was disappointed to have a third boy. Philip wished the baby to be called Martin but she remembered the brother who had been lost at sea and heard the suggestion with foreboding. Philip thought her fears absurd. His great-great grandfather, Martin Shepheard, a contemporary of William of Orange and the great Duke of Marlborough, had died aged ninety-four. No one wanted to live longer than that. Pasqua herself had seen his tomb by the west door of Happisburgh church.

He had his wish and, wearing Lady Webster's fine christening robes, Martin was baptized in their new chapel with one of Susanna's daughters as godmother. He grew into an exceptionally beautiful child with enormous blue eyes and fair curly hair. So much younger than the rest of the children, his parents were absolutely devoted to him and his love and care enriched Maria's life and did something to bridge the gulf between her and Philip.

Madame was less pleased. She had been shocked to hear that Maria was expecting another baby and now advised her to recruit her strength by drinking water in which fir tree tips had been boiled. She asked a London shop to send her some wild cat skins especially imported from Norway which Maria must place flat on her chest every night. These, however, were palliatives. What was fundamentally at fault was their entire way of life. She had seen an advertisement for a house for sale near the sea at Runton. It had a fir plantation in front of it which would provide both medication for Maria and protection from the east wind. If Maria would only sell her sapphires, she herself would advance a thousand pounds towards its purchase.

This particular advice was disregarded. Not, however, some that came from a very different quarter. Anxious about the children's education and knowing nothing of Catholic schools, Philip consulted one of the visiting priests from Yarmouth. Loyal to his order, the priest advised that the boys should go to the Jesuits at St. John's, Beaumont, and Helena to the Convent of the Sacred Heart, Roehampton.

So when they were eight and ten years old, Phil and Helena set out with their father to London. It was Boat Race Day, 1893. Never again would either of them think of the Boat Race, of the Thames sparkling in the cold spring wind and the crowds hurrying over Putney Bridge, without remembering also a sense of desolation which no experience in later life could either obliterate or match.

Neither of them had lived away from home before, neither was prepared in any way for the banishment and boredom which stretched in front of them, year after year, until they were eighteen. The cab took them up Roehampton Lane. Once they reached the Convent a nun opened a bolted door just sufficiently wide to admit them. Helena said a brief, paralysed goodbye to her father and Phil in the dim vestibule beside a lamp which flickered before a statue of Christ whose delicate fingers pointed to his red heart; the burning symbol of the love of God.

When they had gone she was taken behind a screen in another room and told to remove the clothes she came in and change into convent uniform. After that she was accompanied upstairs to a dormitory where her portmanteau was examined for unsuitable toys or books. Then a lay sister ran a fine comb through her hair, replaced her blue ribbons with navy, and suggested that it would be less worldly if her curls were straightened by pulling them away from her face.

In truth, no child could have been less worldly than Helena. She had never been to London nor imagined that any city bigger or grander than Norwich could exist. She had been brought up in the country in the company of her brothers. She was familiar with bows and arrows and birds' eggs, shotguns and fishing rods, with the pale wash of the winter morning and the sun setting over harvest fields. But she understood nothing whatsoever of the interests, values, or even the vocabulary of rich and fashionable girls. She was spontaneous, direct and loving, utterly baffled and indeed terrified by the coldness and rigid self-control practised by the nuns and inculcated into their pupils, the deliberate stripping of natural identity in order to manufacture not an individual but a type.

To this end every minute of the day was mapped out, every action supervised, freedom regarded with as much distrust as emotion. Letters were read, drawers searched, diaries confiscated and friendships discouraged. Victorian prudery combined with religious puritanism to produce a regime whose implications went far deeper than the rule that each child must wear a canvas robe to hide her body when taking a bath. The nuns deliberately cultivated a remote and distant manner. They gave the impression that they were a special creation, some superior species suspended between men and angels. They never spoke of their homes, their Christian names or their birthdays, referred to food or admitted to illness.

At the time Helena could not make out exactly what was wrong. Like other children in similar circumstances, she was teased by a contradiction that she felt acutely but could not formulate. In later life she realized that such an absurd flight from humanity made a mockery of the Incarnation, and hid the very truth the Order had been founded to promulgate. She also came to understand that the goodness in human nature can transcend even the most misguided of systems. Affection, kindness and genuine spirituality squeezed through the tight mesh that separated the nuns from the world Christ died for. Helena learnt much and made friends who were to last until the end of her life.

But that was in the future. Now she had pathetic scraps of letters from Phil, as homesick and heartbroken as herself, written on soggy grey paper with torn edges, barely legible and ill-spelt, opened by the nuns and handed to her without comment.

No one knew anything at all about Maria Pasqua. The nuns casually wondered why it was that the quiet little creature from Norfolk with beautiful manners spoke such excellent French through her tears, and hoped that she would recover sufficiently to do them credit at the next concert. Helena kept her mother's history to herself. She was frightened even to think about it in case her companions should discover the truth and spoil with their laughter the sunsoaked years in Italy and the dancing road to Paris. She knew that the very appearance of her aunts Charlotte and Betty would provoke polite contempt and the thought of the arrival of Uncle Sam in his old clothes bearing his digger made her feel sick. Yet she was ashamed of her shame because she knew whom she really loved, why she loved them and the worth of each.

At Abbots Hall Maria Pasqua grieved for her children. Yet she accepted her separation from them as part of the pattern of existence, something as fixed and unalterable as the tides. Only once in all the years Helena was at Roehampton did she visit her, sitting among the apple-green elegance of the pillared eighteenth-century parlour where from the centre of the room a nun watched to make sure that the girls wore gloves and that no undeclared object passed between parent and child.

Maria felt that Helena was someone else's daughter, some stranger's child, and if they could not speak about anything that mattered they could barely communicate. So the hours for which each had so passionately longed trailed off into banality

111

and even boredom. Maria forgot to give Helena the picture of a chaffinch which Martin had taken two days to colour and even the shortbread made according to Mrs. Compton's recipe was received in the knowledge that it would be put into a locked cupboard to be distributed later. She never visited Helena again, and Philip did nothing to encourage so expensive an undertaking.

The convent then owned some of the most valuable acres in London, a lake, large meadows which were cut for hay, and a working farm reached by means of a tunnel under Roehampton Lane. These places were forbidden to the children, who were restricted to gravel walks and the playing fields. Except for brief glimpses on summer feast days, they might not have existed. Once a year, however, at Rogationtide, since the Church directed that growing things should be blessed and animals demonstrated to be the work of God's hands, the school was allowed to visit the farm. Wearing a white dress and veil, Helena followed in procession, taking tiny steps in the dark tunnel beneath the road where the carriages drove so godlessly to Hammersmith Broadway. Once the other side, the smell of incense mingled with manure, wax candles with damp straw, the high notes of the nun's singing with the lowing cattle and the restless stamping of hooves on cobbles. The pigs grunted in their sties and a boy in brown corduroy trousers held a young calf by a piece of rope. Helena was happy. This she understood. The rest of her life at school was pretence.

Madame de Noailles thought so too. No doubt the fact that Lady Georgiana was buried in the convent cemetery would provide some comfort to Helena; all the same it was very wrong to send children away to boarding school. Most of what they were taught was utterly useless. Even boys, at least in their early years, were far better off instructed by a governess at home, as the career of her distinguished friend General de Horsey demonstrated.

Maria, of course, had heard of the charming and genial Padre Agostino, that wonderful monk whose preaching filled Santa Croce as it had not been filled since Savonarola? He had founded an orphanage at Pisa but unfortunately his bank had failed and she was helping him financially in memory of dear Miss Roche. It was imperative for Phil to leave those unhealthy swamps near Windsor where he would surely die of congestion of the lungs. She herself would write to the head master of Beaumont and suggest that Phil came to Hyères to stay with the Padre, who for a small sum and his keep, was willing to teach him religion and Latin.

Madame's advice was not taken, and in a year or two Samuel went off to join Phil at school, leaving only Martin at home. Nana and the French governess were sent away and his parents looked after him themselves. This was an economy measure. Farming was not paying and the school bills were high.

When she learnt of these retrenchments Madame was furious. What Philip blamed on the times she put down to inefficiency. She had provided Maria with a richer dowry than Lord Granville had given Lady Georgiana and Philip had thrown it away indulging his ruinous hobby. From the very beginning he had sacrificed Maria's health to his own selfish tastes, buying a property nine miles from the coast when he knew that she was only really well by the sea. Why had they not taken Runton House with its healthy fir trees when she had told them it was on the market? Now they were paupers. She had thought over the whole matter very carefully and there was only one course of action which would save them. She would give Holywell Lodge to Maria on condition that the entire family spent the summer there and came out to the South of France to join her for the winter months.

Philip replied coldly that he had not touched his wife's money and enclosed an account from her stockbroker. Maria tried to explain that Philip would never give up farming, nor leave Norfolk, not even in his coffin. As for her, she had to remain there for the sake of her children, particularly Martin.

This was true. Martin was no nursery child like the others. He shared his parents' life in a way they had never done. Seated on a pile of cushions he ate breakfast and luncheon with them in the dining-room, was dressed by Maria in the morning, bathed, read to and put to bed by her at night. Missing the others, feeling the cheerful pictures on the nursery walls mocked a deserted room, she poured out all her love and care on her youngest son.

As undemonstrative as ever, Philip shared her devotion. He showed Martin how to fish and to ride, cut him whistles, cleared a path for his hoop, and in the outhouse by the orchard wall tested the rope of his swing. He gave him lessons, ruling double lines for his letters, teaching arithmetic out of old-fashioned books and how to read from a manual which had survived from his own youth. Every day they sat together at his desk, and every day Philip would mark the progress made in his neat pencilled hand.

Not so sensitive as Phil, nor so introverted as Samuel, Martin was a happy child and the centre of his parents' attention. The image of the son lost at sea faded from Maria Pasqua's mind. She remembered only old Martin Shepheard sleeping full of years on the cliffs at Happisburgh.

Abbots Hall

Erpingham Church

Helena Shepheard, aged seven

Phil Shepheard, aged twelve

Samuel Shepheard, aged eight

Martin Shepheard, aged five

Helena lived for the holidays and the time when she and Phil were together at home again. Phil was the most like Maria Pasqua in looks and temperament. Vivacious and amusing, he was very sensitive, with an appreciation of poetry and the world of the imagination. With that he combined his father's love of the countryside and all its pursuits. Only eighteen months separated him from Helena, and they were close companions. They read together in the bookroom, contrived to rob Samuel of the best parts in their nursery plays, went fishing, rabbiting and boating on the river.

About half-way through the holidays, however, Helena would wake to a dull pain and the consciousness of approaching doom. From then onwards she followed her mother from room to room, watching everything she did, dreading their parting. At night she would cry and hold her mother's hand, imploring her not to send her back to Roehampton, begging her not to allow Madame to make her conspicuous by writing to the nuns. Maria understood these feelings only too well. Temperament and experience, however, led her to suppose that we are all victims of circumstance, that our lives are shaped by events beyond our control and against which it is hopeless to fight. She could do little more than to counsel patience.

During these years Madame de Noailles continued to be extremely busy making plans for the orphanage which she intended to found in conjunction with Padre Agostino. The exact situation was as yet to be decided but it was to be called

St. Mary's Orphanage in compliment to Maria Pasqua, and the girls were to be brought up as nearly as possible like the Blessed Virgin herself. Consulted, Maria was not quite sure how this either was to be ascertained or put into effect, so she was grateful to learn that for the moment all Madame required was the drawing up of a wholesome diet sheet and the costing of each item. She herself considered that the orphans would thrive on bread and cheddar cheese, milk puddings, boiled beef twice a week and suet puddings three times, with the left-over slices eaten cold for breakfast next morning.

It was not, however, to be expected that Madame could be for ever deterred from writing to the convent about their educational methods. Fortunately for Helena, the long-expected letter did not arrive until she had been at Roehampton for some years and had acquired not merely a superficial skill in dealing with her surroundings but a relationship with the nuns that, if never easy, was streaked with affection. When she was summoned to the Mistress General's room she saw at once the familiar black sloping hand and the gold tendrils of the letter 'N' surmounted by its coronet. Who, she was asked, was Helena de Noailles? Who this Padre Agostino? What right had they to dictate to the nuns methods of teaching French grammar?

Helena knew that Madame had long considered French grammars went into unnecessary detail about the past participle. It now appeared that Padre Agostino had worked out a new system of instruction which trod very lightly indeed over participles of any kind, and it was this system that Madame was urging upon the nuns. Madame de Noailles, Helena answered, was her godmother. She had adopted her own mother as a little girl. It was sufficient. As she spoke and saw acquiescence melt the Mistress General's eyes, Helena realized that it was far easier to excuse the eccentricities of a rich countess than to explain why she so longed to visit the farm beyond the tunnel. It was a lesson in worldliness she never forgot.

As time went on and Helena passed her eighteenth birthday and was still at school, Madame became restless. A daughter's place was beside her mother, and unless Helena left Roehampton and came home to help Maria she would cut her out of her will. She was very thankful to hear that Philip did not intend to waste money by having her presented at Court and she now urged that between fulfilling her domestic duties at Abbots Hall, Helena should apply herself to the perfecting of her handwriting and spelling. Lady Burton had suffered so much after Sir Richard's death for want of a good and kind secretary. In Trieste she had had a charming Italian but one who could not bear the English fog. Lady Burton was the salt of the earth and Madame missed living in the same world. What more worthwhile employment for an unmarried girl than to help someone like her?

Maria wrote and said that she would like Helena to spend a year at a finishing school abroad, perhaps at a convent in Rome or Florence. Madame's reply was swift and unexpected. It was *most* inadvisable for Helena to go to Italy at all and a visit to Rome was absolutely out of the question. Did not Maria realize that Carolina was still alive and lived there with her sons? There could be no doubt at all that they would kidnap Helena and demand an enormous ransom for her release.

The letter came as a shock to Maria. So Madame had kept in touch all these years. Her mother was still alive and so were her brothers. Where was Domenico? Dead, or living in some village in the Abruzzi, an old man with grey hair telling amusing stories and perpetually drunk on his own wine? Sharp and rough, not like the white wine grown on the slopes near Montpellier which the Empress had so much preferred to champagne. With what unconscious cruelty had Madame relished her account of the evening she had been adopted, but when it had

happened, and the words actually spoken, she had not understood, she had not even been listening. Had Domenico and his
friends really kept watch to see that Madame fulfilled her
part of the bargain? Would he ever have returned to take her
back by force? She knew that he would not have done,
that he had made for the south as fast as his legs could carry
him.

Maria asked Madame no questions, she did not wish to be
told. Helena was now so fond of the nuns. She should go to
Paris, to the Sacré Coeur and stay in the Boulevard des
Invalides. She wanted her to go, she wished her to see the city
she had reached all those years ago as an exhausted grubby little
creature holding her father's hand but had left in a carriage that
once belonged to a king.

On the evening of 22 January 1901, Philip heard the bells
toll from Aylsham and next morning saw that the flag on the
church tower stood at half mast. A few days later at Roehampton, Helena was making her final farewell to the Mistress
General. Together they felt the vibration of the glass panels of
the door which lead out on to the terrace and opening it, heard
the dull boom of the Tower guns as the old Queen's body was
taken from the Isle of Wight for burial at Windsor.

The September Helena went to Paris, Martin left for Beaumont. Maria had accustomed herself to the absence of the
other children but now, left alone with Philip, the silence in the
house oppressed her. She could not bear to go into Martin's
bedroom or to see the empty chair next to hers in the dining-
room. Martin was only nine, his face still round and childish
and his hair fair and curly. Like his brothers, he was at first
desperately homesick. School, he wrote, was worse than he
thort, he was miserable morning and night, the boy next door
to him the dormintery snorned, would Helena be able to buy
him some sweets in Parice and please, please, would his mother
write? He settled down, however, more quickly than his

brothers had done and by the time Helena returned from France the following year he was sending his parents details of the Eton and Beaumont cricket match and praising the kindness of the priest in charge of the smaller boys.

That spring he caught a cold and told his mother that he was almost well but still coughing. The telegram informing them that he had developed pneumonia and asking his father to come immediately arrived at Abbots Hall on a Saturday morning. It was market day in Norwich and Philip had already left the house.

Maria Pasqua read the message and told the boy to deliver the telegram to the Maid's Head in Norwich. Naturally it was market day, it was always market day for Philip. Wasn't he at the market at Lynn when Ellen was dying, and discussing the price of pigs when she was in labour with Helena? Everything melted away, dissolved before she could touch it. All that pain in the room upstairs on the stifling summer day when Martin was born and Philip was anxious to see that the oats were cut before the weather broke; all that love, all those days and years of care and devotion, all wasted.

Philip was in the middle of his lunch when the telegram reached him. He left the table immediately, telegraphed to Aylsham and set out for Beaumont, arriving at nine in the evening.

Martin took over a week to die. Every day Philip sent a telegram with news and every day there was less hope. He wrote to his wife urging her to come. Martin was crying for her, the boy wanted his mother. Maria would not come. She could not come. Everything was hopeless. She had known that from the moment she had read the telegram. Martin was the most precious thing she had in the whole world, and he would be snatched away from her like everything else, sacrificed for some inexplicable reason like an abandoned Isaac. Her instincts had warned her not to call him Martin. Philip had refused to listen.

She could not see the child, she could not sit by and watch him choke to death. It was not fair to ask her.

Philip wrote again. Martin had received the Last Sacraments. He was very weak. Could not Pasqua manage to come? She collapsed. The doctor ordered her to bed and it was there, on the eve of her forty-seventh birthday, 1903, that she was told that Martin had died. Helena stayed with her mother. Her father, Phil and Samuel followed the coffin to Englefield Green Cemetery near Old Windsor where Martin was buried, as he had asked, in the Jesuit habit. Maria directed Philip to buy a double grave. She wanted nothing to do with Norfolk; she refused to lie at Erpingham with his family. If she could not be with Martin in life, she would in death. Writing in pencil by the light of her oil lamp, she scribbled beside a passage from the ninth chapter of St. Luke's Gospel, 'My boy Martin is dead – Mother'.

Miserably unhappy herself, Helena feared her mother's grief would kill her. Philip returned home, thin and pale and silent. He noted in his diary the time and place of the funeral, and on the following day recorded that they had finished barley sowing. He was unable to communicate with his wife. Once, coming up quietly, Helena was appalled to catch sight of him sitting sobbing at his writing desk. She had too easily seen him through her mother's eyes and until then never suspected that such deep feeling existed in one so reserved and remote. When the holidays arrived and Phil and Samuel had to bring back with them Martin's trunk from Beaumont, she would have done anything in the world to have spared her parents the sight of it.

Maria Pasqua shut herself off completely from everyone and walked up and down by the orchard wall for hour after hour. She thought, as she had so often, of a black-edged, lacy card thrust between the pages of Ellen's prayer book. Gayton Vicarage, it had read. In memory of Annette who had died, aged five-and-a-half, of scarlet fever. 'My beloved,' the Vicar had chosen as his text, 'my beloved is gone down down into His garden to gather lilies.' To gather lilies in His garden. As a young woman, alone in the drawing-room at Gayton, she had wondered how the Vicar and his wife had endured their loss. Now, walking slowly by the rusty door from Norwich jail, past the bee hives and the swing waiting motionless for a boy who could never come, she understood that they had no choice.

Madame was extremely kind, not by a single word reminding Maria of her warnings about the unhealthy swamps near Windsor. She consoled her as best she could, telling her that since Martin had committed no sins on earth, he would surely be waiting for her in heaven. Besides sending a picture of Lord Kitchener for Helena to copy and show to her mother in order to distract her mind, she forwarded a substantial sum so that the family could spend the entire summer by the sea at Cromer. For Maria Pasqua's sake Philip agreed to go, but he insisted upon taking his armchair with him.

SIXTEEN

The children had spent their summer holidays at Cromer since they were quite small. Maria Pasqua loved the sea, even the North Sea, and enjoyed the atmosphere of hotels, the warmth of the sun through conservatory glass, the smell of potted plants and cigar smoke, the constant bustle and the gossip about new arrivals.

In those days Cromer was a fashionable resort, and Maria liked seeing and hearing about people who had formed part of the background of her girlhood. She remembered complicated relationships, knew which branch of a family had married into another and the style and status of the children. Philip was not in the least interested either in Burke or the Almanach de Gotha. It meant nothing to him that the Empress Elizabeth of Austria was staying at the Bath or the Duchess of Marlborough at the Hotel de Paris. Unlike Helena and Pasqua, he did not particularly wish to see the Empress walk out daily to the bathing machines then in charge of a young man called Blogg, later to gain fame as the coxswain of the Cromer lifeboat. If the Empress sat for hours drying her long yellow hair in the sun she was entitled to do so; at heart all he wanted was to return home and supervise the harvest. Maria enjoyed the pier with its slot-machines, crowds and concert parties. She loved the nigger minstrels and the large smiles with which they greeted her children. Above all she loved the theatre.

Madame had considered the theatre frivolous and meretricious. To Maria it was magic. When he married, Philip had finished with that sort of amusement. She had hoped to see plays in London, he was reluctant even to take her to the theatre in Norwich.

In the years that followed Martin's death Maria relied very much upon the companionship of her daughter. Sometimes they managed to slip away from Cromer and visit the playhouse at Yarmouth. On one such occasion they saw *The Merry Widow*. When they came out Helena happened to glance back and to her horror caught sight of her father in the crowd. They were forced to wait until he joined them, when Maria Pasque falteringly remarked how much she had liked the performance. Looking very grave, Philip told them that when he used to go to the theatre in the old days plays were no doubt coarser, but he thought that the double meanings he had noticed in *The Merry Widow* far more harmful and indelicate than anything he had seen in his youth. He was shocked to see how much they both appeared to have enjoyed it.

Left to herself, in an environment which suited her, Maria would never have surrendered to the streak of melancholy which underlay her natural gaiety. She was quick to puncture solemnity in others and particularly in Helena, who as a girl was inclined to draw gloomy conclusions about the human condition. Once during the interval of a play her mother said softly, 'Regardez donc, vous venez justement de manquer de voir les tragedies de la vie.' Helena looked up quickly and saw two women who were desperately trying to pass each other. One was on the way back to her seat and both were very stout.

Outside her home absurdity delighted Maria. Inside it Philip's mere presence extinguished her laughter as surely as a covered cage silences a canary. The love and care of Martin had for a time forged a closer link between them. When that snapped, Maria's resentment at the restraints her husband put upon her and her inability to find any pleasure in his company overwhelmed her. She spoke constantly of her own country

and how she yearned to see it again and longed to put her
hands on the warm rocks and watch the little green lizards
basking in the sun. She was convinced that if only she could go
back to Italy she would to find her mountain peak in the
Abruzzi without any difficulty.

She took to growing orchids and spent longer and longer
alone in her greenhouse. Madame became more anxious than
ever about her health and was certain that it would take an
immediate turn for the better if she would but adopt the open
air cure. This involved the construction of a special summer
house and the purchase of a tricycle. Half the day must be spent
riding up and down the drive on the tricycle, the other half
resting in the summer house, which was to be built of boards
three-quarters of an inch thick and covered with brown paper
upon which Helena should paint sepia drawings. A partition
was to be made in the middle so that Maria could lie on a sofa
either on the east or west side according to the direction of the
wind. A large cheque arrived from France. Maria bought a
revolving summer house but there were no partitions, brown
paper or sepia drawings. The tricycle came and was occasionally used by Philip to spare the expense of ordering the
carriage.

At that time Philip was very perplexed about the future of his
sons. Phil did not seem to have any particular gifts or desire to
do anything more exciting than to read and to potter about the
countryside fishing or shooting. Philip was very glad, therefore, when after long doubts and hesitations his eldest son
decided to join the regular army, and he was even more pleased
when Samuel announced that he intended to become a doctor.

This news galvanized Madame. She had just read in the
Royal Agricultural Review that children brought up on *good*
milk seldom became drunkards. Surely Samuel would like to
assist the late Cardinal Manning in his wish to diminish
drinking? If so, he should train not as a doctor but as a *vet*,

thus improving the health of mankind by improving that of *cows*. She had long been thinking of selling some land on the Downs near Holywell Lodge to help Armenia. But if Samuel became a vet she would leave the land to him in order to build a convalescent home there for animals. Would Philip kindly telegraph yes or no?

The answer was no, and very soon Samuel was enrolled as a student at St. Thomas's Hospital. The brothers were utterly different. It is impossible to say what was born in Samuel and what was made, but he was a quiet boy, rarely able whole-heartedly to enjoy what life offered. Overshadowed by Helena and Phil, he had been very attached to Martin, whose depend-ence had brought out all that was best in his character, and he took his death badly. The roots of his discontent, however, lay farther back and were grounded in jealousy of Phil.

Phil was the eldest, he was the one who was always given the best gun, the first pony, the new pair of skates. He was the one who would inherit Abbots Hall, run the farm, shoot the coverts, fish the river and collect the honey from the hives. Samuel would be banished to earn his living elsewhere.

His school reports made him out to be dull compared with his brother. In fact he was just as intelligent and had a real gift for drawing, covering notebook after notebook with animals, plants and buildings, all minutely observed and beauti-fully executed. Unfortunately, in those days, such accomplish-ments were considered neither part of the school curriculum nor worthy of praise.

It was a good-looking but rather moody boy with a sense of grievance who accompanied Philip to London to enter the hospital and find suitable digs. A Catholic priest, a friend of the family, had suggested that one of his congregation, the widow of an impoverished Irish gentleman, would be only too glad to let a room in her house to a medical student. Philip was not to know that she had an exceptionally pretty daughter and that his well-intended choice of lodgings would influence Samuel's entire life.

Madame had not taken offence at the rejection of her schemes. She begged Maria to come to Hyères, or if she could not, to allow the children to visit her. Phil would have liked to have gone but he was cramming for the army. Samuel said he could spare a week and would accompany Helena provided that she got someone else to see her home.

Having agreed to go, the prospect of meeting Madame again filled them both with a mixture of alarm and excitement. Although they had not set eyes on her since they were children, her influence had penetrated their very bones and their mother's childhood was as real to them as their own.

Letters containing complicated and sometimes impossible instructions arrived almost daily. Helena must bring two pots of Vinolia cream and two of pomade, a loaf of Maria's home-made bread and four parlourmaid's caps. Samuel was to take with him a barrel of soft roes just like the ones which had done her chest so much good in the yacht off Yarmouth at the time of his birth. He must also bring a brace of partridge and take the utmost care not to allow them to get *cold* before packing them in a *hamper*, not a box.

Since it was April this last request could not be honoured. Nothing was said about swinging hammocks, but Helena was warned that for the sake of her eyes she must on no account sit anywhere else but with her back to the engine, nor must she bring more than one frock as Madame had cool clothes already waiting for her. This alarmed Helena considerably since she dreaded being forced to dress in a white tunic with a girdle as her mother had had to do. Maria went with her into Norwich and with the utmost difficulty they obtained some pale, loose frocks intended for the wives of officers serving in India.

Maria Pasqua

The last letter arrived the day before departure. Helena was
to promise that on no account would she accept any invitations
to five o'clock tea as it was well known that people caught
influenza not so much from physical contact as from the miasma
which hung about in the air after sunset.

SEVENTEEN

At Hyères station Helena and Samuel found that a carriage had been sent to meet them and they drove through beautiful scenery to Madame's house, Villa Mont Claire, at Costebelle. When they got there they saw it was a very large building with shuttered upper windows and grounds which reached down as far as the sea.

The coachman set them down at the front door and drove with their luggage round to the back. There was no one about and little to disturb the silence except the sound of cows tied up outside the windows and munching hay. Nervously they approached the front door and looked in vain for a bell or a knocker. In the end Samuel was forced to bang very hard on the wood with his knuckles. After a long time Madame's maid, Paula, appeared and conducted them through long corridors to a distant wing of the house where they found bedrooms prepared for them. Madame, Paula said, wished them to rest until one o'clock, at which time she would see them for luncheon.

Telling Samuel to wake her at least half-an-hour beforehand so that she could get ready, Helena fell into an uneasy sleep. At the appointed time Paula came to fetch them and they were led back to the other side of the house, shown into a very large room and told to wait. They noticed that all the door handles were covered with dark blue silk, tied on with ribbons of the same colour. Helena was just asking Samuel what he thought was the reason for this when Paula's husband opened the door and Madame de Noailles herself glided slowly into the room.

She was now nearly eighty and had aged considerably since Helena and Samuel had last seen her when they were children at Eastbourne. The skin lay in soft folds above her eyes and her mouth had shrunk inwards making her nose more prominent than ever. She was dressed as they remembered her, in a long, loose robe of figured silk and she carried an ivory fan. She kissed both her visitors and then stood back and looked at them, nodding her head like a mandarin and fanning her face with a slow, gentle sweep.

Luncheon was an ordeal, and Helena and Samuel were very relieved to be told that they must not expect to see their hostess again until the same time the following day. Next morning they went to look at the sea and then explored the garden. The mimosa was in full bloom and an old wisteria covered the stables, its enormous mauve flowers blending with the intense blue of the sky. They watched the cows brought out and tethered under the windows which were opened very wide so that their healthful breath could penetrate far into the downstairs rooms.

Near the front door Helena saw some curious little wooden buildings. When she opened one of them to see what was inside she realized to her great surprise that they were, in fact, portable earth closets converted into hen houses. The seats were still there but perches had been erected above them and on these the hens roosted at night.

At noon, Madame appeared, accompanied by several dogs, including a huge Great Dane. Chairs were placed near one of the cows and they all sat down. A man came forward and milked the cow into glasses, brandy was added and they all drank.

Madame seemed delighted to have them with her, but if she had aged in body her mind was as sharp as ever and her eyes as quick, so that every meeting was an ordeal. One of the first things she looked at was Helena's shoes. Fortunately Helena had listened to Maria's warnings and brought with her the flattest and widest pair Norwich could produce. She had heard that once when a young cousin of Madame was staying with her she had put on what were her best and most expensive shoes with high heels. Madame had asked her to show her one of them. She did so. Madame promptly threw it into the fire, demanded the other and did the same with that.

She subjected them both to a constant barrage of questions about politics in England and the state of the economy. She inquired in what estimation Browning was held and whether scholars considered the paintings of Alma Tadema correct in their archaeological detail. Knowing her low opinion of boarding schools, they were much afraid of betraying their ignorance and once at luncheon nearly did so. Madame spoke of the stupidity of one of her guests who did not know the date of the Battle of Salamis. Samuel quickly changed the subject and looked up the date at the first opportunity. The next day he said innocently, 'Did you tell us that you had a guest here who actually did not know the date of the Battle of Salamis?' 'Yes,' Madame replied, 'but do you know it yourself?' After that she appeared to think that they were not too badly educated.

The servants were terrified of her, and she used often to sit on a chair watching them while they had to climb trees barefoot to cut off branches. One of the old gardeners told Helena that he had lost his wife in a volcanic eruption and that he was very poor. Once when she was going round the garden with Madame she told this old man to weed a border.

He did not seem to know the weeds from the flowers and pulled up some tulips. Madame said bitterly, 'That's right, go on pulling them up!' The poor old man thought she meant it and went on pulling up the tulips. She yelled, 'Imbecile!' and to Helena's disgust struck his hand with her stick. He gave a cry of pain and then sobbed. He was often hungry and used to look with longing at the cream given to the Great Dane.

Samuel was thankful that he had agreed to stay for a week only. There was nothing to do except to walk by the sea or in the woods, and he found the company of Madame an unbearable strain. There were so many subjects which were unsafe to mention. At any moment, however guarded one was, a mistake could be made and the consequence would be a severe lecture or vehement tirade. Madame, however, liked him. Writing to Maria, anxiously waiting for news at Abbots Hall, she said, 'Samuel reminds me so much of you, can I give him greater praise?'

Helena dreaded being left by herself for another three weeks but there was no help for it. In general Madame was very affectionate. She was a lonely old woman to whom neither her wealth nor her schemes had brought happiness and she had the intelligence to realize it. She walked arm-in-arm in the garden with Helena and told her to call her 'grandmother'. One day she said she had something to show her and took her upstairs to her bedroom.

Wonderingly, remembering a child who had once pushed a chair to a dressing table and poked small fingers into pots of facecream, Helena sat down by the bed. Madame gave directions to Paula who presently returned carrying a cardboard box. Madame told her to place it on the counterpane and to go away. She then opened the box and removing some tissue paper asked Helena to look inside. There, neatly folded, Helena saw some beautifully worked baby clothes, the satin ribbons, ivory with age, threaded round the little cap and bodice. They had been intended, Madame said, for her own child, who had been stillborn. Overwhelmed by inarticulate pity, Helena thought that if the baby had lived she herself would never have come into the world, and her mother would have remained an illiterate, poverty-stricken peasant.

Madame dwelt a great deal on the past, speaking constantly of Maria Pasqua and her longing to see her again. She told

Helena what she had felt when she first caught sight of Hébert's picture, and how the expression in the lovely eyes had determined her resolve. She described the difficulties she had encountered in carrying her scheme to its successful conclusion, Domenico's behaviour on the evening he brought the child to her in Paris, and the happy life they had spent together before Maria married.

After Samuel's departure Helena was not expected to be idle, and to her dismay Madame suggested that she wrote letters at her dictation. These included some to Lord Cromer, written at some length, as Madame wished to give her younger half-uncle the benefit of a detailed programme she had devised for the economic recovery of Egypt. Others were addressed to philanthropists or prominent politicians. One such had been directed to Henry Hobhouse M.P., beginning with the daunting paragraph:

Sir,
Having seen your name mentioned as one present at a meeting of fifty Liberal Unionists on the question of Protection, I venture, on the assumption that you are a relative of the Sir John Hobhouse to whom Byron dedicated the 4th canto of Childe Harold, to hope that you may possibly sympthise with a side of the question which has not, I think, as yet been brought forward.

It was not all work; friends of Madame sometimes called at the house and, thinking she might be lonely, invited Helena back to their homes. One family who owned a villa close by called *Les Hirondelles* frequently invited her to their house and once or twice Helena met a French doctor who was staying there.

One evening, towards the middle of her visit, Helena was surprised to be sent for by Madame. When she reached her room and sat down, Madame said that she wished to speak to her very seriously indeed. She had noticed that Helena always put on her best hat to go to *Les Hirondelles* and seemed to look forward very much to her visits there. She was sorry to have to tell her that a French doctor had that day come to see her and had asked for Helena's hand in marriage. She knew, of course, that she would not wish to marry him and had given him his *congé* in no uncertain terms. It would be a most dreadful thing for her ever to get married and to leave her mother.

Helena was astonished and did not know what to believe. She must, Madame continued, reluctantly forbid her to visit *Les Hirondelles* again. At this point she rang the bell and told Paula to bring in the hat she had left out in her bedroom. When it arrived Helena's heart sank. It was made of plum-coloured straw with a heavy textured veil. If it did not fit, Madame said, she could put cotton wool inside the brim, but she must wear it whenever she went out. Although it was not her wish for Helena to meet people, she must have some recreation and she hoped a daily airing in the carriage would be a suitable diversion.

So it was done. Wearing the hideous hat, Helena sat by herself in the carriage and watched the countryside roll by. She was very lonely and the face of the nice fat coachman lengthened when he considered how sad it was that such a pretty creature had no one to talk to.

Paula and her husband came from the Black Forest. She had two children whom she had to keep concealed at the back of the house so that they were not seen by her mistress. She had been employed by Madame for fourteen years, and she told Helena that things had become even more difficult now that Madame was older and that her temper had deteriorated. Helena witnessed one outburst of rage.

It happened one day at luncheon. Madame suddenly screamed and pointing to the door, yelled, 'I'm struck blind! I'm struck blind!' Helena could not think what had happened but looked towards where the hand was pointing and noticed that one of the silk covers had fallen off the door handle, which was of some bright metal. The maids who were serving huddled together in fright. Helena called for Paula and when she came into the room Madame screamed out that she had been blinded on purpose. While Paula quietened her, Helena was able to tie the cover over the door handle once more. In the silence which followed, Madame appeared to be rather ashamed of herself. She explained at great length that her eyes were exceptionally delicate and could not stand the reflection of any bright object.

To Helena's disappointment, the charming and genial Padre Agostino did not put in an appearance, but General de Horsey used frequently to come to tea. The General had ridden in the Charge of the Light Brigade at Balaclava; his sister had married its commander, Lord Cardigan. Helena poured out the tea and silently listened to the conversation of the two old friends, both so full of reminiscences and allusions to a vanished age. The General treated Madame with a ceremony and politeness which Helena knew she would never witness again except on the stage of a theatre.

A few days before she left, something happened which further opened Helena's eyes to the strange mixture of the good and the disagreeable in Madame's character.

She had been much surprised to hear, at certain times of the day, sounds of the Latin office being chanted in a room not far from her own. The voices were those of women. Puzzled, she spoke to Paula who told her that Madame had very kindly given refuge to twenty nuns who had been turned out of their religious house by the French government. One morning Madame introduced the subject herself by asking Helena if she had seen the nuns because she was anxious, before Helena left, for her co-operation in a little scheme designed to find out if they really were good women.

Helena was to put them to the test in the following manner: Reverend Mother and two other nuns were to be asked to go to one of the reception rooms where Madame herself would be present but concealed behind a curtain. Once there, Helena was to tell the nuns that Madame de Noailles wished to help them and was prepared to give them money so that a house for the community could be bought in Italy. There was, however, to be a single condition attached to the gift. Madame, herself a Protestant, would give the money only if the nuns were willing to say that the Epistle attributed to St. James was not by him at all and thus formed no part of the New Testament.

As straightforward as her father, Helena was dismayed by the proposition. She was also young, dependent and too frightened of Madame to dare refuse. Hoping that the nuns would stand firm, conscious of the listening figure behind the curtain, she delivered her speech in careful French. Reverend Mother clasped her hands with joy and tears came into her eyes. Alarmed, Helena repeated with some emphasis the condition about the Epistle of St. James. When Reverend Mother really took in what the provision was, she shook her head sadly. She was very grateful to Madame de Noailles, but she could not say what was not true.

Madame was rather disappointed that the nuns had not fallen into her little trap. Nevertheless she bought them their convent.

Helena went once with Paula to Carqueiranne to see the house where Madame spent the summer months. Paula said that she expected the household would move there soon and described the extraordinary progress they made from Hyères. The whole removal was made by road. The cows came first led by the men, then the hens shut up in their portable earth-closets which were carried on poles, two men to each fowl-house. Madame herself brought up the procession, carried on a litter. Paula said that crowds stood at the roadside to watch this strange cortège which took place twice a year.

So Helena's visit came to an end, and although Madame seemed sad at parting from her, she was not sorry to go. She would miss the nightingales and the orange trees, but she had found Madame very difficult and realized a little of what her mother must have gone through.

EIGHTEEN

In January 1905, on his twenty-first birthday, Phil sailed for India from Southampton taking with him an express rifle which Madame had sent him from London on the condition that he wrote articles on tiger shooting for the newspapers. He had at first been gazetted as a second lieutenant in the Norfolk Regiment, but got himself transferred to the Essex because the Norfolks were at that time stationed in England and he was determined to go abroad.

Much as Phil loved Abbots Hall he had found life at home increasingly difficult. His father's old-fashioned outlook had hardened over the years. Clinging to provincial habits which belonged more to the eighteenth than the nineteenth century, Philip did not realize what a domestic tyrant he had become.

Pasqua and he went to bed at nine, so must his children. He took one candle only from the row waiting for them on the hall chest, so must they. For fear of fire he never read in bed. Neither must they. He had had an almost obsessive fear of fire since he was a child and was always anticipating an outbreak. For this reason he trained his children and domestics in fire drill and installed loud bells at both front and back of the house so that the farmworkers could be summoned and, bearing buckets from the pond, speedily form themselves into a human chain.

He never suggested that Phil should join him in the small quantity of whisky he drank in the evening. He said he hoped and supposed that his son did not take it. In fact, Phil had a bottle in his bedroom. Once, and once only, was this routine broken. When Phil was thirty and a captain and at home on his last leave before going to the front, his father suggested that they might have a glass of whisky together. Less than a finger was poured out and they both drank in silence.

Maria and Helena missed Phil's companionship greatly. Madame sent Maria a card table so she could divert herself playing écarté in the winter evenings. Convinced that yet another winter at Abbots Hall would kill her, she badgered Lady Florence Dixie into sending Maria a vicuna rug exactly like the one the intrepid Lady Florence had slept under in Patagonia with only a saddle for a pillow.

It was, however, Madame herself who was the sick woman. Characteristically she remained silent on the subject, but in 1905 Paula wrote to tell Maria that she had a growth on her breast. She lived for three more years, hoping to the last that Maria would come and visit her. It was sad to be old without the companionship of a relation. Surely she could come, and Philip too? She sought his advice about the hospital she was intending to build and she wanted to know if she should have the eruptions on her cows washed with rosemary tea. She would provide an Italian cook and parlour maids from Padre Agostino's orphanage to look after them. If Maria felt tired in the evening she could be carried upstairs to bed as she herself was. Only let her come before it was too late.

Philip would not budge. Madame wrote to say that she had heard that a miracle had taken place near Lahore, something very like the conversion of St. Paul. She wondered that Phil had not mentioned it. But the large handwriting was fainter and signature barely decipherable.

In 1908 Paula wrote to say that Madame had asked for Maria to be photographed with her hair down like the Madonna, just as she remembered her as a girl. She spoke constantly of the happy times they had had together. Madame was being kept alive on champagne and milk. Would Maria pray that the end would be peaceful?

Philip maintained that since Madame was so ill, no useful purpose would be served by Pasqua going all the way to Hyères. For once Maria threw off the almost fatalistic inertia which bound her to her husband's will. She set out for France alone. Hardly had she left the house when a telegram arrived, 'Stop Maria. Noailles.' It was their last communication. By the time she reached Carqueiranne Madame was unconscious.

She left twelve wills, and an estate worth, even in the undervalued currency of the time, over a hundred thousand pounds. Eventually these twelve wills were whittled down to two, one written in French, the other in English, with a codicil to each. About these two wills the legal battle was fought. There were visits to Philip's solicitor in Aylsham market place, long depositions taken by his clerk in the dining-room at Abbots Hall, letters to London attorneys, and huge bills to counsel. It took seven years and a series of complicated lawsuits involving many claimants before the case was resolved.

In all the wills Madame had left money to Maria, and in some Holywell Lodge or other properties in England and France which she owned. One of the many problems was to decide whether the wills were to be executed under French or English law. If one of the codicils which revoked certain legacies were proved valid, then as far as her property in this country was concerned, Madame had died intestate and the English property would devolve upon the heir-at-law. Maria's legal position as heir, however, was not clear. What had happened that evening in the house off the Champs Elysées had been a private transaction. There was no entry of adoption in the French register, and in any case adoption by an English person could not be recognized in France. Even if it were decided that Madame was a French subject there remained legal difficulties about a French person adopting an Italian national.

The case was finally decided by an action in the Chancery Division of the High Court in 1915. By that time the old world had passed away and Phil was on the eve of embarkation for the Dardanelles. The Solicitor-General complained about the length of the proceedings and consigned the English will to the wastepaper basket.

The document finally proved was a worthy testament to Madame's eccentricity. In it she left Holywell Lodge as an orphanage for the daughters of clergymen of the Church of England. The chief purpose of the home was to 'give abundance of health for the use of the spirit'. Religious instruction was to be 'equally far removed from Calvinism on the one hand as from Ritualism and Sacerdotalism on the other'. Book learning was to be a secondary consideration. All competitive examinations were forbidden. No study was to be permitted before breakfast or after six o'clock in the evening. No child under ten was to be taught any arithmetic except the multiplication tables.

Vaccination was forbidden. Every candidate for admission was to be examined by two fully qualified phrenologists and no girl was to be admitted to the orphanage who was suspected to be deficient in conscientiousness or firmness and 'upon this point the reports of the phrenologists shall be held to furnish conclusive evidence'.

A rather sad codicil, which must have been added after Madame discovered the nature of her disease, was declared invalid. In this she left money to build a sanatorium on the Eastbourne Downs for young women with cancer of the breast. No doctor who practised animal vivisection was to be allowed near the patients.

Eventually Maria received a small sum of money from the will and in addition a cousin of Madame, who considered her to have been unfairly passed over, gave her a portion of the value of Holywell Lodge.

Philip had curtly noted the fact of Madame's death in his diary together with the information that he went to Norwich that day to sell wheat and barley. Maria's reactions were more complex.

The dragon was dead, a restraint was lifted, a shadow dissipated. As long as Maria remained in the South of France she was buoyed up by the change and excitement. A friend who saw her at Hyères described her as running about and enjoying herself like a lark. Once she had made the psychological effort to escape Maria wanted to stay away longer, but Philip would have none of it. He sent her strict instructions to return to Paris and, to make certain that she did so, despatched Samuel to join her there. Helena went to meet them at Norwich station. Her mother looked radiant. She was wearing a Paris hat and carried an enormous bunch of flowers given to her by the Duc de Mouchy.

It was her last flutter. Norfolk in December is quiet and very cold. Before long gloom enveloped Maria like a shroud. She began to see herself entirely in the role of victim. Madame was gone. There was no link left between Rome and Paris, the dancing Domenico and the little girl who had shaken a tambourine, the smell of paint in the rue de Navarin and Hébert holding her face between his hands. Who remembered now the game of *poisson d'Avril* at the Bellevue in Cannes or cared for the pieces of bright paper she had cut out and given to Madame on her birthday morning when she was in bed at the Grand Hotel des Anglais? Domenico had sold her in vain, the bargain struck for nothing. The tide of life which had once swept her so gallantly forward had left her stranded in the depths of the country with a man who would hardly talk to her and whose interests she could never share.

She hated the English winter. She hated the dark days and the cold winds and Philip's meanness in allowing only one log of wood to be burnt on the fire at a time. If he left the room for an instant, she would dart to the woodpile, put on another log and try to kick it into burning up before he returned. But he always noticed and would inquire severely whether it was Helena or her mother who had behaved so wastefully. He now instituted what he called a dark hour, insisting that it was an old Norfolk custom. The servants were forbidden to bring in the oil lamp until one hour after dark and Helena and her mother sat round the table in resentful idleness.

It was at this time that Maria took to calling Philip '*le vieux*'. She said that according to the Bible, man's days were three score and ten so that *la délivrance* could not be far off. Soon there would be no more dark hours, only olive trees and al- mond blossom, soaring mountain peaks and the fierce shepherd dogs with spiked collars. Never by word or look did Philip show that he minded her attitude or was aware of it.

Only a few of the friends of her girlhood remained. Pauline von Hügel had died comparatively young, the Comptons were gone; Miss Francken, the pianist who had accompanied her so long ago on her journey to the Pyrenees, and the Coventry Patmores remained in touch. The poet was dead but Mrs. Patmore and her step-daughter Bertha lived at Lymington. Maria, unable now to make the effort to leave home, used to send Helena to stay there in her stead. Mrs. Patmore tho- roughly approved of Helena and would have liked to have made a match between her and the son whom she and the poet had called Francis Epiphanius.

Helena was fond of Piffie but did not wish to marry him. She was exceedingly hard to please and frightened of making a mistake. She met few people. Her parents rarely called upon new arrivals and almost never entertained. Helena had not been taught to dance and, in any case, had never been invited to a single ball. The mothers of eligible young men in the neigh- bourhood had no desire to have a Roman Catholic daughter-in- law and did not, therefore, encourage visiting. Intelligent,

Helena in 1912

Edward Watkin at about the time
he met and married Helena

Phil in 1914

Samuel in 1916 or 1917

Samuel in old age, in the grounds of Abbots Hall

artistic, and endowed with an unusual independence of mind and spirit, Helena found the children of her father's shooting acquaintances for the most part conventional and dull.

If he had any particular friends, Samuel did not bring them home. He had done very well at his medical studies but his personal life was in shreds. Madame had been wrong in her estimation of him. He was more like his father than his mother. He had all Philip's reserve and direct, rather simple emotions. The girl he loved so violently, and indeed for the rest of his life, was called Eileen, the only daughter of his landlady. She was unusually pretty, tall, well-proportioned with a head of red-gold hair.

She had been well educated at the Sacred Heart Convent in Dublin and Samuel adored her. Since Philip disapproved of young men who were extravagant when they had their living to seek, Samuel's allowance was not large. But whenever he could afford it he took Eileen out to supper, to Saturday tea at Fullers, to the Zoo, and to hear the German band in the park. He was single-minded and utterly devoted, and at some time between his third year and his final examinations he asked her to marry him.

He may have been remarkably good-looking and he may have had a most attractive voice, but he was a younger son with no estate to look forward to, no prospects other than those attained by his own exertions. Perhaps Eileen did not really care enough to marry him, or at any rate not sufficiently to wait until he was able suitably to support her. Perhaps she thought she could do better for herself. She turned Samuel down in favour of a young captain in the Indian Army and set sail for Calcutta.

With his family, Samuel was silent and tormented, confiding in no one. A photograph of Eileen, torn into small pieces in one fierce moment of pain and rejection then carefully glued together like a homemade jigsaw puzzle, stood on his chest of drawers; it was to remain there for the rest of his life. Neither

Helena nor Maria Pasqua dared to ask questions. Within a month of Samuel passing his final examinations, Phil came home on leave. It was 1909 and the last time the brothers were to meet. As soon as he had spent his prescribed period as a houseman in a London hospital, Samuel put into effect his resolve to leave England. He had twice seen Eileen who had returned to her mother to have her first child, and he wished to get away as far as he could from an impossible situation.

In George V's coronation year he was appointed medical officer to an expedition setting out for the remote Choco valley in Colombia, and had hardly left Aylsham before Phil returned again from India for five months leave. Far away, camping in the damp heat by an alien river, Samuel inquired about his wall flowers and his fishing rods, the honeysuckle he had planted and his hazel-nut saplings. Threatened by malaria, snakes and vampires, travelling by canoe, living in huts made from the bark of palm trees, he heard of his brother's homecoming and resented it. If Phil borrowed his skates he must make sure the blades were covered with vaseline afterwards. He wasn't going to have them spotted with rust, nor would he allow Phil to touch anything else that belonged to him. Let him find that his locked boxes had been tampered with and in future it would be better to keep the ocean between them.

The day that Phil returned to India, a dejected Helena went over to Sheringham with her parents to be present at the blessing of the Jesse window in the new church there. This window had been given by a rich woman in gratitude for a brilliant first gained at Oxford by her only child.

Edward Ingram Watkin was then aged twenty-four and had known Helena and her family for over a year. As a boy he had been removed from a conventional preparatory school and sent to a much smaller establishment run by the Revd. the Marquis of Normanby in his home, Mulgrave Castle, Yorkshire. He had then travelled with a tutor on what amounted to the grand tour of Greece and Italy before spending five terms at St. Paul's School and going up to Oxford.

Attracted by the love of beautiful ritual and the medieval past, he had become an Anglo-Catholic in his teens, but began to fear that the Church of England would be unable to stand firm in the face of the rising tide of secularism and the assault upon the Creeds. Staying at Lambeth Palace, he took the opportunity to put his misgivings before the Archbishop of Canterbury. Often accused of undue deference to the great, Archbishop Davidson nevertheless took the trouble to talk at some length to a schoolboy who asked him a question which, but for the obvious sincerity of the inquirer, might have appeared impertinent.

If, Edward asked in the course of a walk in the garden, the dignitaries of the Church of England were allowed to question the Virgin Conception and the Resurrection, what guarantee was there that it would still be teaching those doctrines in future years? That kind of guarantee, the Archbishop answered, the Church of England neither claimed to give nor believed should be given; such an attitude towards religious truth belonged, not to the Reformed Church, but to Rome. To that Church Edward went.

His mother, now a widow, was a daughter of Herbert Ingram, the founder of the *Illustrated London News*, who had been drowned in a steamer accident on Lake Michigan while in America covering the visit of the Prince of Wales and, so it was said, at the same time privately negotiating to buy up the waterfront at Chicago. Edward's great-uncle, Sir Edward Watkin, sometimes referred to as the Second Railway King, held the controlling interest in the Channel Tunnel Company and had entertained Gladstone with a champagne luncheon in the excavations, which stretched for over a mile beneath the sea.

The gifts of imagination, commercial acumen and drive that enabled such men from comparatively humble origins to be so successful in public life, had been transmuted in Edward's case into an absorbing love for religion, history, literature and philosophy. Engrossed in the world of ideas and protected by wealth from the tedium of ordinary existence, he devoted his time to reading or walking about the countryside identifying plants and admiring nature and ancient buildings with an intensity derived from Walter Pater.

Such was the man Helena wished to marry, and the engagement perplexed Philip. This strange and gifted youth was six years younger than his daughter and did not seem to be under the necessity of taking up any profession. He did not know one end of a gun from the other or a fishing rod from a landing net, yet they said that he was reading Macaulay almost before he could speak. It was rumoured that he could translate from five languages and was already half-way through a book on apologetics and planning another on the philosophy of mysticism. He did not seem to notice what he ate and often went about in the shabbiest of clothes, with lost buttons or broken shoe laces, carrying an old bag which contained a flora, the Latin psalter, a thermos of tea and the missal in the Dominican rite. Pasqua had heard that he had been arrested as a spy when staying in Spain and narrowly escaped a night in the cells at Biarritz.

He had the most unexpected family connections, like A. N. Hornby, the former Lancashire batsman and captain of England, mentioned in a poem Philip had always liked by Francis Thompson about long-dead cricketers bowling to ghostly batsmen at Lords: *As the run-stealers flicker to and fro, to and fro, | Oh my Hornby and my Barlow long ago!* Philip was getting on now himself; he hoped that when he was a ghost Edward would look after Helena, although why she wanted to leave such a good home he failed to understand.

In sables and diamonds, Mrs. Watkin drove over to Abbots Hall to discuss the marriage settlement. She was a little, thin, energetic, plain creature with the speedwell blue, protuberant Ingram eyes. Maria looked at her and thought how extraordinary it was that Helena's future mother-in-law should be the goddaughter of the William Paxton who had designed the Rothschild château at Ferrières, the very place where Hébert's portrait of her had hung, and how strange that Edward should be in correspondence with Pauline's brother, Frederick von Hügel. How twisted the threads of life were, how careful Helena must be of this woman, how desperately she would miss her when she left, how much she wished that Phil would hurry up and be a major and retire and live at home as he said he would.

They appeared, Mrs. Watkin was saying, to live in a quiet manner in the country, so she would finance the entire wedding herself and it should be at Brompton Oratory as she liked the architecture. She had already ordered the material for the dress, a heavy brocade hand-embroidered with gold and silver thread.

Philip was glad to be spared the expense, but Maria felt anxious. Was Helena to be under the thumb of an equally capricious version of Madame de Noailles? What Edward's mother gave she could as easily take away.

So it proved. Lonely, reluctant to relinquish a son whom she did not understand and was incapable of unselfishly loving, Mrs. Watkin did her utmost to stop the wedding. Determined not to be bullied by the power of his mother's purse and showing an unexpected grasp of business matters, Edward completed the arrangements on his own. In the autumn of 1913, wearing a plain blue frock, Helena married him at Cromer. Philip gave his daughter away, the future historian Christopher Dawson was best man, Maria Pasqua and a brown and lean Samuel were the only other witnesses.

That afternoon, *en route* for Italy, Helena and her husband caught the London train. An hour or so later Samuel went in the same direction intending to meet Eileen before going on to the School of Tropical Medicine. The South American expedition was over. He had returned with some knowledge of conditions in a little-explored part of the world and with a new species of orchid which Kew named after him. After seeing Eileen and attending his medical course, he hoped to set out on his travels again, this time to the Ashanti River in what was then the Gold Coast.

Edward and Helena spent the first part of their honeymoon in Rome where they received the Pope's blessing, and then travelled in the Abruzzi. There they stayed in flea-ridden inns, examined old churches and searched for Maria Pasqua's mountain. They went to Scanno and to Sora because Maria thought that long ago she had heard the names spoken. Every day Helena sent a picture postcard to her mother who, sighing, tied the growing pile with pink ribbon and awaited her release. The following August war was declared.

NINETEEN

Philip's attitude towards the war was completely different from Maria's. She felt all the detachment of the peasant who does not care if he is governed by the King of Naples, the House of Savoy or the Pope provided he is left alone. She was cosmopolitan; the anti-German hysteria struck her as absurd. How could people like amiable, elderly Miss Francken be turned into monsters overnight? She hated all war and did not think that any cause in the world was worth the life of her children. 'Let the Germans come,' she scribbled by the side of the Epistle to the Galatians.

Philip, on the contrary, wrote immediately to the War Office offering his services, but since he was seventy-six they were not required. Of his two sons, the professional soldier was the least belligerent. In temperament more like his mother, Phil did not share the general hatred of the Germans nor the crude jingoism which sustained the nation in a barbarous, prolonged and unnecessary conflict. As soon as the news of the declaration of war reached Samuel on the Gold Coast, however, he set sail for England. His was not to reason why: if his country needed him, he could fight as well as Phil.

It was plain to all that even if Edward had been able or willing to hold a rifle he would have proved more of a danger to his own side than to the enemy. His sole contact with the armed forces took place in the village of Cawston where he had gone one afternoon from Sheringham to look again at the beautiful old church with its magnificent rood screen.

So absorbed was he in the glories of the medieval carving, that he failed to hear the vicar's key turn in the lock. When dusk fell and he found he could not get out he climbed the tower stairs and, once on top, waved his handkerchief vigorously in the direction of the village. A local inhabitant who saw him was convinced that she had caught a spy and instantly gave the alarm. Before long a body of soldiers surrounded the church, a flustered vicar produced the key and the blunt, incredulous fingers of a baffled sergeant fumbled amongst the flora, the Latin psalter and the Mass in the Dominican rite before taking a protesting Edward into custody.

For most of the war, however, Helena and Edward lived not in Norfolk but in Oxford and it was there, in February 1915, that Phil came to meet Edward for the first time and to say goodbye to his sister. He had embarkation leave before setting out for an unknown destination. Although they shared an interest in botany, Edward had always found it difficult to keep a conversation going with Samuel. Phil was easy to get on with, and the three of them had a great deal to say to each other.

The last days of Phil's leave were spent at Abbots Hall. He had no illusions about his chances of survival. He told Maria Pasqua that if he did not return she must not grieve for him: he had led a very happy life but he thought that the best of it was over. Walking with her by the chapel he picked up a stone with a natural mark on it like a cross which he had noticed before. This he placed by the chapel door telling his mother that if he did not come back he would like it to be left there in his memory. It remained in the same place for fifty years, known and cherished, until the time came when the weeds crept up and the grass covered it. Perhaps it lies there still.

Phil fought in the famous 29th Division and that June was killed at Gallipoli. His father saw the messenger boy walking up the drive with the dreaded telegram and went out to intercept him so that Pasqua would be spared the shock of opening it. The son who was least like him he had loved the most. She did not need to ask any questions after she had seen his face.

Phil's colonel wrote to say that he minded his death more than that of any other of his officers. Phil, he explained, had been with his company three hundred yards ahead of the main portion of the brigade and had been hit when jumping out of the trench in an attempt to prevent the men on his left flank from retreating. His body and those of the sixty-two men of his company who had died with him were never recovered.

In her New Testament, beside the account of the Passion, Maria wrote, 'Phil died, killed at once, so they say'. She sent word to Helena who was recovering in a London nursing home from a dangerous operation. There was no comfort in her letter, nothing but a piece of paper with the stark news of his death. Helena wished that she had never come round from the anaesthetic.

Samuel was serving as a medical officer in the Middlesex Regiment, then stationed at Gibraltar. The ocean had indeed been kept between them. Phil passed his brother on the way to the front, but had not gone ashore there. From Gibraltar Samuel tried clumsily to comfort his mother. She should think of the numbers of her countrymen who had in the past been killed by the Turks. She ought to take her mind off things by growing new plants in her greenhouse. Perhaps his father would get her another so that she could have twice as much room. Yet even in death he thought his brother the lucky one. It was a good way to die, at once, attacking from a trench. For Phil everything always worked out for the best.

In the August of that year Phil's few belongings were returned from the Dardanelles. Among them Philip found a packet of love letters. When he realized what they were he made no comment but lit a fire in the cold hearth and burnt them without reading further.

He was, therefore, prepared in a measure for what was to follow. Before long a letter arrived from an unknown woman, the wife of an officer who had been with the regiment abroad. She said that she and Phil had loved each other for many years and her grief was almost unbearable. He had spoken so much about his family and the haunts of his boyhood; the river, the water meadows, the hole near the boathouse where the old pike waited. She asked if she could come to Norfolk and see his home.

For once Philip and Maria were in accord. After long thought they wrote to say that although they could not approve of what had happened, all that mattered now was their shared love of Phil. They invited her to Abbots Hall so that she could see for herself all the things which he had told her about.

Helena had her first child, Christopher, towards the end of the war. Although grudging every moment of his wife's absence, Philip thought it proper that a mother should be with her daughter at such a time and Maria Pasqua spent an entire month away from Abbots Hall. It was a period of anxiety because Helena was very ill, but Maria was surprised at the pleasure she felt in having a grandson.

During her convalescence Helena went to stay on the south coast. One day she went over to Eastbourne and sat for a time near Beachy Head listening to the guns on the other side of the Channel. She found that the intervening years had made many changes. Villas had sprung up and new roads been built and she wondered if it would be possible ever to find Holywell Lodge. Eventually she discovered Meads post office and asked an old woman there if she could direct her to the house. The old woman stared at her with a trace of apprehension before exclaiming that she knew it was impossible but that she looked the image of Madame de Noailles's adopted daughter.

Pleased to be thought so like her mother, Helena found her way past the familiar iron gates to the front door. To her amazement Madame's old housekeeper, Elizabeth, answered the bell. She summoned her husband Albert and soon they were renewing old memories and talking of the days when he used to wait at table, often in fear of Madame's displeasure.

War and litigation had rendered all her plans sterile, the house a purposeless monument to the vanity of human wishes. Elizabeth took Helena to see the rose-coloured emptiness of Madame's bedroom and downstairs into the dust-sheeted drawing-room where as children they had stood in wonder before the Lawrence portrait.

A spoilt picture, an impossible bequest and from across the Channel the sickening reminder of relentless slaughter. Helena thought how right her old Uncle Sam had been. The folly and imbecility of mankind were indeed infinite.

TWENTY

After the war Samuel came home for good. Apart from two days a week spent in Norwich examining ex-servicemen who claimed to be suffering from tropical diseases, medicine was more or less abandoned. He sold Phil's horse and decided that, living where he did, it would be better to hunt the otter rather than the fox. He bought about six couples of hounds and employed a kennelman. As Master he designed the hunt uniform, arranged the programme and provided material for accounts of the season's activities contributed to the press under the pseudonym of 'Chieftain'. He hunted not merely the River Bure but transported his hounds to Stiffkey, Holkham and as far across the county as Castle Acre.

This interest absorbed him. He was only thirty-three and he wished to be absorbed. Eileen's husband had become a colonel but the marriage had broken up. After the divorce she came to live permanently in England. Samuel's religion was as strict and undeviating as his father's. What Eileen had decided, she had decided. There was no help for it now. He could not marry her.

For a long time Philip kept the management of the estate in his own hands. Nothing was changed. Remarkably active for his age, at eighty-three he was still capable of acting as chairman of the bench of magistrates. Maria Pasqua recovered slowly from Phil's death, accepting it more calmly than she had Martin's. But her thoughts were constantly on escape and she persuaded Samuel to enrol her as a member of the Touring Club Italiano. When *la délivrance* came she and Helena would first of all go on a spending spree in Paris and advise each other about hats. Then they would take the train to Rome before going farther south into the mountains where they would surely find her peak.

She never thought of her country in a political context. Its post-war problems, the rise of Mussolini and Fascism did not bother her. In her mind Italy was a dream country whose inhabitants, forever young, dwelt by mountains and streams and played pipes in the cool of the evening.

She was frightened of old age. She had resented the changed texture of the skin on her arms, the droop of the eyelids, the puckered ear lobes and goose neck of middle life. Her whole spirit rebelled against the prospect of becoming gradually like her husband. She found it hard to accept that people no longer looked at her, that her body was plump and her nails had ridges in them. The black silk which in her youth had set off her features to such advantage was now the detested uniform of the elderly, of those whose lives were finished, who were expected to sit and smile while other people amused themselves. One afternoon she was by the river watching some boys fishing and one of them asked his companion where he had left the tea. He answered that he had put it down on the grass not far from the old lady. Surprised, Maria looked round and with piercing dismay realized that the old lady was herself. It was useless to tell her that the fine bone structure of her face remained. She thought of herself as she had been; nothing could compensate for what was gone.

Helena wrote from London that she and Edward had been round the French Room at the Tate and that she had caught sight of a picture of a girl whose expression reminded her of her daughter, Perpetua. It turned out to be the portrait of Maria entitled 'A Greek Captive'. The reminder served only to increase Maria's gloom. What prophetic vision the artist must have had, what inner eye to know that the little model would remain a prisoner for life.

She could not believe it possible that *le vieux* could live so long. Year followed year in miserable monotony and still *la délivrance* did not come. She had read that when the doors of the Bastille were unlocked at last, the prisoners refused to walk out. There was such a thing, she told Helena, as being in prison for so long that when freedom actually arrived people did not know how to make use of it. Suppose that should happen to her?

If Philip realized her feelings he gave no sign and his attitude towards his wife remained unchanged. One summer day when he was over ninety, Helena was sitting with her mother in Madame's garden shelter. It began to rain and they saw Philip slowly crossing the lawn with a large umbrella. It was tea time and he was afraid that Pasqua might get wet. He remained vigorous. Once when Helena was there for lunch and Samuel in Norwich, a maid rushed in screaming from the kitchen with her clothes burning. Instantly Philip got up, seized a rug, smothered the flames and calmly treated her for burns and shock as if he were still that young doctor in Gayton and not an old man of over ninety-two.

His health failed only very gradually. He did less, became more deaf, slept longer in his armchair by the fire or sat for hours in the sun. Once in her tactless youth, Helena had re-marked how horrible it must be for him to be old and unable to do things any more. 'Oh,' he had answered, 'but what a time I have had.' He seemed content. His affairs were in order, there was only one thing on his mind and that was the future of Edward, Helena and their five children.

During the war Edward's mother had fallen victim to a Cana-dian colonel and had married him beneath a triumphal arch of swords at Holy Trinity, St. Marylebone. Philip knew human nature. Unless Edward played his cards skilfully his step-father would scoop the pool, and where would Helena and the children be then? His mother and Colonel Heakes were living in a villa on the island of St. Helena, of all remote and unlikely places; and there the old lady would get more and more under her husband's influence.

Philip wondered how the children were to be educated. When they had been on speaking terms Edward's mother had offered to send her grandson, Christopher, to Eton but his father had refused because the school was no longer Catholic. Then there had been a cousin who had been prepared to defray the expenses of Stoneyhurst but the offer had been turned down because, unlike Pasqua, Edward did not approve of Jesuit education.

Edward could not afford now even to live quietly on the Welsh property he had inherited from his father – and it was not as though he were idle. He worked hard enough behind the study door in his blue house at Sheringham. He had translated a long history of England in the nineteenth century by Halévy and just published a volume of essays entitled *The Bow in the Clouds* – a reference to the Flood, of course. Excellent stuff, but too learned for Philip, and unlikely to earn enough to save them from drowning.

He must alter his will. As things stood now, after provision for Pasqua Samuel got everything, but that must be changed. The estate would have to be divided equally between the two children. It was the fairest way. St. Helena. How well he remembered his old nurse threatening him with Boney. Boney will come if you go on crying. Boney will get you if you stay out in the garden any longer. And before that it had been Old Noll. Old Noll will catch you, his grandfather's nurse had said to him. Well, he was ninety-three but no one could say that his memory had gone or that he was not in his right mind.

The value of land had fallen as low, so he had heard, as £25 an acre. He would leave the property in trust equally to Samuel and Helena, the amount in the trust to be decided by the value of the land at the time of his death. That wouldn't be much. Pasqua must have the income of the trust during her life and the contents of the house absolutely. When she died Samuel could buy Helena out and Helena's share of the capital must go to her children.

It was the best he could do. It was a pity that Sam, Charlotte and Betty had left everything to the bishop to build a church at Aylsham. But they couldn't have known that Helena would need help. Philip sent a message to his solicitors in the market place and without revealing its provisions to his family, signed his final will in May 1932.

He celebrated his ninety-fourth birthday with a shooting party. Helena came to visit him the next day and thought him very tired. That evening he recorded her visit in the diary he had kept for over sixty years. It was his last entry.

A nurse was not brought in until almost the end. She was disconcerted to be told when she asked for her patient's teeth on the first night that if she wanted them she would have to pull them out. Philip had no particular illness; he just faded away early in the morning of the last day of the year 1932, and was buried among his own people at Erpingham near the tower of the church where he had worshipped as a boy. On the way back from the funeral, amidst the leather and thumb-marked chromium of the undertaker's car, Maria Pasqua told Helena that she never wanted to see her again.

Samuel had been absolutely outraged at the provisions of his father's will. Abbots Hall was his life. He had been born there, he expected to die there and he loved each stick and stone of it. He was familiar with every inch of its fields, gardens and river; to threaten the integrity of the property was to threaten his whole existence.

He bitterly resented having to suffer for Helena's misfortunes. *He* had not married, *he* had not had five children, *he* had

not been such a fool as to quarrel with the woman who held
the purse strings. Hadn't he come back from the war to look
after his ageing parents? Hadn't he done his best to help his
father run the estate, then arranged for the farm to be let?
Why should he be expected to *pay* to get back what was his by
natural right? How did he know what capital he would have
by the time his mother died? Soon they would have to pay the
death duties: suppose when the time came he could not buy
Helena out even at £25 an acre? Something might have to be
sold. He was terrified by the thought of losing his hounds.
The hunt was his creation. Life would be empty without the
brown uniform with its badge on the cap, the van bowling
across the county to Binham, the printed programmes and hand-
written pedigrees, the stench of offal at feeding time, the
barking, the growling, the clanging doors of the kennels.

Her husband's death together with the provisions of his
will stunned Maria Pasqua. Samuel had explained that he would
have to give half the value of the estate to Helena. A primitive
fear from some far depth of her experience rose to the surface
and overwhelmed her. She would be poor again. She would be
hungry, dependent, a beggar. Things had not worked out in the
least as she had imagined they would. Nothing was going to
be changed after all. There was never going to be an escape
because there were no doors left to open. Samuel was right.
Helena must have come over with hard luck stories, worrying
her father with insinuations of bankruptcy and tales about a
wicked mother-in-law and coaxed him into leaving her money.

Maria had been betrayed by her own daughter, stabbed in
the back by the very one who was to have been her partner in
pleasure. All those years of hope, plans and bright dreams had
once more dissolved into nothingness. Everything was finished.
Nobody could be trusted, they all let you down in the end. The
only people in the whole world who had cared for her for her
own sake and not asked a single thing in return had been the

Sisters of Charity. Domenico, Hébert, Jalabert, Bonnat, Madame, Philip, her children, they had all wanted something, all used her, exploited her, squeezed her dry.

Fifty years since the evening she had given birth to Helena in Ellen's room at Bridge House, Maria sent her own summons to the Market Place.

She, Maria Pasqua Shepheard, widow, of Aylsham in the county of Norfolk, wished her body to be taken back to Italy and to be buried in Rome; if that were not possible she wanted to lie beside her little boy Martin at Egham. She revoked all former wills and declared that she left two thousand pounds to be divided between the convents of the Sisters of Charity in London, Paris and Rome provided that they hung up a copy of one of her portraits in a conspicuous place with a short history of her life written by her son, Samuel, appended to it. The rest of her estate including jewellery, furniture, pictures and all her personal possessions whatsoever she left absolutely to her son, Samuel, and should he die before her everything should be sold and given to the Sisters of Charity.

What about Helena and her family, the lawyer asked, surely the marriage settlement drawn up by Madame de Noailles had arranged for the capital to be put in trust for all her children? The stiletto was drawn; it hovered and struck. That had been left to her discretion, Maria answered. Let him write down that her daughter was already amply provided for.

Christie's arranged the sale of some Chippendale chairs and William and Mary chests, a Georgian wine cooler, a Guercino drawing, pictures by Ibbetson, de Vries and Trevisani, together with a miniature by John Wright of Ellen's mother in a white dress. It contained a lock of her hair. So the death duties were paid, and the crisis was over. There would be no disbanding the hunt, no leaving home, no begging in the streets or settling in dingy lodgings near the station at Cromer.

But there was no Italy either, no spending spree, no joyous

flight to the sun, nor warm rocks and emerald lizards; not even an expedition to London to buy clothes. Electricity was installed but the routine established by Philip barely changed. Maria looked after the aromatic plants that had replaced the orchids in her greenhouse, watering the pelargoniums with a long-spouted can, pinching leaves and savouring the scent of lemon and orange, rose, ginger, and peppermint. From the dining-room window she watched Samuel take a swarm of bees and asked if hounds had found at Blickling Mill. Philip's empty chair was removed, the logs on the fire were a little larger and the electric light allowed to burn in the hall in case Maria stumbled on her way to bed. Age had overtaken her, and with age infirmity.

She sat before the fire or on the bench which Philip had loved, facing south by the front door near the lemon verbena, and with thick wooden needles knitted very slowly width after width of striped blankets. Perhaps Samuel would give them to the women in the cottages. Blue was for Madame and the Mediterranean and Miss Roche, red for Holywell Lodge and Bournemouth and her friend Pauline, orange, yellow, and brown were for her life with Philip, the long street at Gayton, old Simson's eagle on his bookplate, their coming to Aylsham and the nursery walls. Poor Nana had had a stroke. Everyone said that there would be another war. What a pity Philip had not lived long enough to know that Alfred Cooper's boy had been made First Lord of the Admiralty.

Samuel bought her a bloodhound puppy which she called Thor but he grew too large and boisterous to remain indoors and had to be banished to the kennels. Maria loved him and every day she would ask Samuel for Thor to be freed in the garden so that he could put his paws on the window ledge and she could feed and talk to him.

Helena refused to believe that the mother she loved so deeply and with whom she had shared so much, really did not wish to see her. She went to Abbots Hall and was denied entry. It was not in her nature to force herself on anyone; nor did she complain. As reserved as her father, she grieved inwardly and waited.

In 1937, while Edward was working on *A Philosophy of Form*, his mother died. Although they were reconciled on her deathbed she had, as Philip had foreseen, left everything she possessed to her husband and it was only through the generosity of the nuns that Helena's children were able to remain at Roehampton.

On New Year's Day, 1939, Maria Pasqua wrote, 'I am alone here,' besides the First Epistle to the Corinthians. Six months later Samuel wrote to say that she was very ill.

When Helena arrived at Abbots Hall she found her mother extremely weak and realized that she had not long to live. Together with Samuel she looked after her during the day and knowing that she would hate a strange nurse, asked the gardener's wife to sit with her at night. Maria accepted Helena's presence as if she had never left home.

Gradually she became feebler. She still moved her hands when she spoke but with little short gestures. Grapes were the only things she liked and she kept a bowl by her bed, fumbling for them with thin fingers and eating very slowly. She remembered the names of each of Helena's children and asked for news of them. Sometimes she forgot that she was in Norfolk and that the landscape outside her window stretched flat and far over the cornfields to Aylsham. Didn't Helena think the Pyrenees were very beautiful? Oh, how beautiful it all was. Sometimes, but rarely now, she spoke of the past. It was good of Madame, wasn't it, to bring her up as a Catholic. She'd been entirely in her hands. No one would have known. But she'd promised Domenico and kept her word.

The local priest came to give her the Last Sacraments and when he came downstairs Helena could see that he was deeply moved. He hoped, he said, that when the time came for him to die he would be half as ready to go as she was.

One day, after she had been there for three weeks, it became clear to Helena that her mother had not many hours to live. She sat by the bed with Samuel, overcome with sadness. It no longer mattered how she looked, Maria was past noticing the expression on her face. It was a hot afternoon and the silence was broken only by the distant call of the rooks by the gate and the sound of Thor persistently howling in the yard. Over the door the carved angel brought long ago from Worsted church looked down serenely upon the three of them, and from its oval gilded frame the unnaturally large eyes of Hébert's little girl followed every movement in the room. Maria was quiet but her breathing had become very shallow. She died, her hand in Helena's, towards five in the evening. It was July 14th and the French were celebrating the fall of the Bastille.

Maria Pasqua was buried, as she had asked, not at Erpingham but with Martin at Egham. One of the workmen on the estate made the coffin of plain unpolished oak and the hearse was accompanied by four men who had worked for the old people for years and had loved them. Everything was as Maria would have wished; the church at Egham in the Italian style and for the ceremony the parish priest joined by a Jesuit from Beaumont.

As they passed through the streets of Egham on the way to the cemetery a few men lifted their hats and some people paused in their shopping just to wonder, perhaps, whose funeral it was. Helena looked at them and thought how little they could know of the strange and unusual life of the woman who was being taken to her grave.

EPILOGUE

Samuel Shepheard lived on alone at Abbots Hall for over thirty years. War was declared the summer that his mother died and he joined the Royal Observer Corps, spending many days and weary nights searching the skies for the sight of enemy aircraft crossing the coast. Hunting almost ceased but he bought in hounds, hoping that when the war was over he would be able to continue as Master. Agriculture prospered and he kept a bailiff in the old farmhouse by the water meadows. At the Hall the servants were not replaced. When the war came to an end he employed one person to come in for two hours a week.

He slept on an iron bedstead in the old night nursery with a window open summer and winter. The birds nested on top of the cupboards, scattering the floor with wisps of hay, feathers and lime droppings. Eileen's torn photograph shared the chest of drawers with a picture of the Sacred Heart and a bald animal he had played with as a child.

He cooked for himself, eating in one of the inner kitchens by the warm Aga on a table covered with a copy of the *Eastern Daily Press*. The dining-room was used as an estate office and the table from which his namesake liked to raise a ceremonious Christmas glass to his mother was piled high with bills, estimates, income tax returns, and copies of the *Field* and the *Lancet*.

He kept the drawing-room windows shuttered and the door locked, leaving everything inside exactly as it had been on the afternoon of his mother's death. When Helena's grandchildren came to see him he would unlock the door and take them in there and, not knowing what to say or how to amuse them, wind up the ancient polyphone. Both young and old were anxious to please but each was stiff, shy and wary of the other. Samuel feared that his visitors might ask to keep the polyphone, touch or damage it. They were puzzled by the perforated metal discs but too frightened by the abrupt voice and bewildered by the gloomy rooms and locked doors to venture to ask how the music came out or who had played it long ago in this mysterious house where people so close to them had lived and died. So they sat upright on the dusty cushions of the window seat listening with sad little faces to a creaking rendering of the 'Blue Danube' while the light from the half-opened shutter fell on Ellen's rosewood worktable and the photograph of Madame sitting stiffly between the lilies and the labrador.

There was not enough light to pick out the blue and gold of the scalloped corner cupboard in front of which Phil had posed for a photograph with his hand on his dress sword. Only those who had known the room in the past would have realized its extent and what it contained. The long glass which had once so clearly reflected the white, wasp-waisted frock Helena had brought back triumphantly from Paris acted now as a dark pool, suggesting in its depth a multitude of objects extended in infinite space.

Upstairs all the bedrooms except Samuel's were locked. No one went much into the bookroom, and only Helena on her rare visits crept along the linoleum covered corridor to look at the pictures on the walls of the old nursery. Under the roof, locked attics were crammed with tin trunks and broken furniture, collections of birds' eggs, seashells and specimens of snakes. A stuffed kingfisher lay sideways on the floor next to odd dolls, bows and arrows, draught boards, washstands, Maria's embroidery frame, medical implements and a rusted pair of skates.

Samuel was glad now that he had not been able to marry Eileen or been trapped by any of the local women who had set their cap at him. Wives were always interfering, tidying up and generally meddling. He was happy, he was independent, he could do what he liked with his own, and if he felt lonely he did not say so. He saw Helena occasionally, but although in a way he was fond of her, it was the fondness of someone who loves his hands and feet just because they are his and he cannot be parted from them. Old grudges surfaced constantly, and he spoke of her with the resentment of a man who had been once cheated and was taking good care to see that it never happened again.

His nephew Christopher stayed frequently in the house, said Mass in the chapel and fished the river. Some of Samuel's nieces stayed too; others came over for tea by the Aga in the kitchen. He was kind to them all, but with the conditional amiability of an ageing dog who growls at the faintest suspicion that a hand might be moving in the direction of his bone.

Every single thing in the house was his, from the broken chairs in the attic to the Queen Anne bureau in the drawing-room, from the merest pamphlet on the Tichbourne Claimant to his great-grandfather's translation of Juvenal. The silver was safe in the strong box at the bank together with his mother's sapphires, the diamond earrings, the jewelled cross once belonging to the Duc de Poix, and, of course, the corals. There were so many corals, how much his mother had loved them. Helena cared for them too. She was waiting no doubt for her mother's jewellery and so were her daughters. But he wasn't going to give them away; if his mother had wanted Helena to have them she would have said so.

He was still Master of Hounds, but as time passed meets became rarer and the field gradually contracted to a handful of faithful followers. Hounds grew slow and almost never found.

The last of them went in 1964. She was called Dainty and he hated shooting her. The venture was over.

The smell of mice, formerly slight, now began to pervade the house. In Maria Pasqua's bedroom grime covered the oval glass of Hébert's portrait and the wings of the angel crumbled gently into a fine powder. Above the staircase dust settled like thick velvet on the antlers of the buck Phil had shot in Baluchistan and the photographs of Eileen as a girl became indistinguishable from those of Samuel's mother. In the hall below, spiders made their home in the lantern of the *Peggy* and a film of dirt obscured the masts in the long panoramic picture of the fleet at anchor in Yarmouth Roads.

Gradually the garden crept up to the house. The clematis darkened the dining-room windows and climbed the wooden balcony to Philip's dressing-room. The flower borders merged with the paths and the tree-lined drive became overgrown with seeded lupins so that no one used the carriage entrance any more. Arches of berberis and forsythia, thickets of broom and bamboo thrust forward unchecked, and a tangled mass of roses completely covered the gate from Norwich jail and blocked the way to the outhouse where Martin's swing hung rotting from its hooks.

As year followed year the gardens themselves were swallowed up by the wild. Nettles and brambles crept in from the surrounding fields. Chickweed, docks and red poppies invaded the asparagus beds, thistles took over from delphiniums and phlox and buttercups from aubretia and pansies. But in the spring the violets that Maria Pasqua had planted still grew in profusion by the front door and the daffodils flowered in the grass. Samuel was careful to keep the path to the greenhouse clear enough for the boiler to be attended to and his mother's lemon verbenas and aromatic geraniums flourished in their warm and watered corner.

Helena's death in 1972 at the age of ninety, although

expected, came as a jolt to Samuel. He was infirm himself, with severe arthritis and a bad heart but he never complained and nothing would have induced him to leave his home. However, he knew now that he would have to make up his mind finally about the disposition of his property.

He started to jot down notes on the backs of the few Christmas cards he received. No flowers; flowers at funerals were a great waste of money. The Catholic Prisoners' Aid Society; his mother had given generously to that every year. The Sisters of Charity, of course, and the little blue nuns who used to call at the house. Those were good causes. And St. Joseph's Hospice for the Dying, they'd see that the priest came in at the end. Then there was Eileen's daughter, the last of her children. He remembered how unhealthily fat her first baby had looked when he had seen him on Eileen's lap in her old mother's front room at Ealing before he had left for South America.

There were no Shepheards left, no one in the male line to leave it all to. That was odd, considering old John Shepheard's large family. He would give something to Helena's children but none of their husbands had the least idea how to farm, they were all bookish like Edward. It would have been all right if Phil and Martin had lived. Christopher was a monk, nothing could be done in that direction.

There were the Macks. They had had to sell their precious Paston; they'd all had to go, but he was still at Aylsham. His father used to say that old Mack had got rich by foreclosing on mortgages; Susanna hadn't liked that, but she hadn't liked her husband either. Philip Mack's sons had done very well in the war, one an Admiral and two in command of destroyers, but they weren't Shepheards. The name would die out. What had persuaded Alfred's son to take Norwich as his title? Probably because all those Coopers had been born there. Anna Cooper had been called after old Marsh's second wife, Anna Candler, but no one cared about that now, once one was dead no one bothered any more. Money left to relations was money wasted.

'Ship's lantern from *Peggy*, lost in 1772', he wrote on the back of David's *Flight into Egypt*, Norwich Museum. Also lantern of Rush the murderer. And the box of butterflies from Colombia. The horns of Phil's buck and the head of that animal he had shot in Burma were nothing very special. They could be sold with the rest. Strangers could have them.

He wouldn't have his family tramping about his house and touching all his things when he was dead. Greedy, female hands with painted finger nails going through his drawers, spying eyes looking at his letters and account books, poring over albums from Erpingham and Gayton, opening boxes containing small private things that belonged to him and to him alone. He would destroy what he could while he could. He took his mother's cream and orange wedding dress from the iron chest in the hall and stuffed it down the throat of the Aga. She had kept the letters which had passed between Philip and herself during their engagement in the figured mahogany cupboard by the clock. He removed them and placed them on the ashes of the wedding dress. But he was tired, the impulse died. He would get on with it later.

In the May of 1973 a Norfolk solicitor received a letter in an unknown hand. His correspondent lived at a place called Abbots Hall, Aylsham, and wished to make a will. The lawyer drove over and was astonished at what he saw. The drive was apparently impassable and the garden looked like something from a film of the Sleeping Beauty. Puzzled, he left his car by the side of the house, walked round and knocked doubtfully on the peeling brown paint of the front door.

The old man who opened it was wearing breeches and a tattered riding jacket. His face was a deep brown and his eyes dark blue. Despite his clothes and his rich, English voice with its Norfolk rhythm, there was something faintly exotic about him. He might have been an ancient Sicilian vinedresser or a fisherman from the shores of the Aegean.

The interior of the house astonished the solicitor still further. If he had not seen it with his own eyes he would not have believed that such a place existed. A Victorian house almost perfectly preserved if one discounted the dirt. When the end came he would get in touch with Norwich Museum, the people there must be given an opportunity to photograph it. Stacks of books, pictures, furniture and goodness knows what else he had not seen. He wondered why the old man lived like that. With land at its present price he must be worth over a quarter of a million.

Samuel had put his affairs in order only just in time. Towards the end of 1973 he had a heart attack and with extreme reluctance agreed to go into hospital. The old house was empty at last, and on December 19th what Philip had always feared came about. The farm bailiff was feeding the cattle on the other side of the road when he smelt burning and saw smoke rising from the roof of the Hall. By the time he had run across and telephoned for help the flames were already leaping from the nursery wing. A small crowd assembled in front of the house and cheered the arrival of fire engines from Aylsham, Reepham, North Walsham and Wroxham.

The trouble was caused by a fault in the electric wiring; a cable had been smouldering under the rafters for weeks. When Samuel was told that through the prompt action of his bailiff the house had been saved, he made plans to sleep on a camp bed in the dining-room so that he could direct the repair of the roof and upper floors. But those about him, seeing the old man lying so still with his knotted fingers folded over his rosary, knew that he would never go home.

He died on the very day of Helena's funeral the year before and was buried on a wild January afternoon in the place he had chosen near to her in Erpingham churchyard. The rain poured in torrents, the trees bent almost double over the open grave and Christopher's voice could hardly be heard above the howling of the wind.

At Aylsham the same wind whistled through the trees of the overgrown drive and here and there lifted the tarpaulin on the roof. In the greenhouse the stove had gone out and past the chapel where Samuel's body had rested the previous night, violent gusts rattled the iron doors of the kennels and scattered old pedigrees, vet's prescriptions and pre-war fixture cards over the brick floor.

In the dining-room Maria Pasqua's workbasket stood where she had left it on the sideboard thirty-four years ago. A tea tray for the mourners lay in a cleared space among the clutter on the table and upstairs in the silence of the old nursery the gallant soldier saluted the huntsman and the girl in blue smiled at the little boy with his hoop.